Tim Mullis

Christ Church

# youth emmaus

# youth emmaus

## For Growing Young Christians

Stephen Cottrell, Sue Mayfield,
Tim Sledge, Tony Washington

Illustrations by Craig Cameron

CHURCH HOUSE
PUBLISHING

Church House Publishing
Church House
Great Smith Street
London SW1P 3NZ

ISBN 0 7151 4988 1

Published 2003 by
Church House Publishing

Cover design by Church House Publishing

Printed in England by Biddles Ltd, Guildford
and King's Lynn

# Contents

*Contents*

# Foreword

In a rarely visited school chapel on a hill above Nazareth there is an unusual statue of Jesus; not the usual infant in his mother's arms, or the classic Good Shepherd or Sacred Heart, or on a cross, but of the Lord as a teenager.

Perhaps because there is silence in Scripture about those hidden years of his life between his encounter with the teachers in the Temple as a twelve-year-old until his adult ministry began, and perhaps because much of our proclamation rightly concentrates on his death and resurrection, Christians rarely imagine Jesus as an adolescent, as 'youth,' or rarely do they reflect upon the implications of a God who is so committed to teenagers that he became one of them – breaking voice, hormones and all!

For him teenagers are neither a 'problem' nor people somewhere in between childhood and adulthood on the way to being 'grown up.' To the Lord they are fully alive NOW. They can be saints NOW!

In a rare insight to his own teenage years, Luke tells us that as Jesus grew 'he advanced in wisdom and in favour with God and people.'

This surely sums up our hopes for all young people, and I have little doubt that *Youth Emmaus*, when used well and led by people who themselves find Jesus irresistible, has real potential to introduce teenagers to life with him, so they can grow the way God wants them to.

Undoubtedly, the need to introduce young people to the Good Shepherd is urgent. If the Church does not care enough about them to do so, then there are plenty of enthusiastic but false shepherds, 'hirelings,' that are prowling about with other things, other lifestyles on offer, most of them tawdry, some of them dangerous, and none of them good enough.

The original *Emmaus* process has been a great blessing. *Youth Emmaus* looks very good. A real love for young people, and much listening, thought and prayer has brought it to birth. Let's use it!

*+Lindsay Urwin OGS*
*Bishop of Horsham*

# Acknowledgements

The authors would like to thank the young people, clergy and youth leaders in the parishes of St George's Barnsley, Bishopston and St Andrew's Bristol, St Thomas' Clapton Common, Bristol Christ Church Mount Pellon Halifax, Holy Trinity Hartlepool, St John the Baptist Kirkheaton Huddersfield, St Mary's Luddenden with Luddendenfoot, St Andrew's Netherton, All Saints Normanton, St Matthew's Northowram, Peterborough Cathedral, the King's School Peterborough, St Mary's Twickenham and St Catherine's Wakefield for their help in the production of this material.

The authors would also like to thank Sheridan James and Tracey Messenger at Church House Publishing for their help and enthusiastic support for *Emmaus*.

*The authors and publisher gratefully acknowledge permission to reproduce copyright material in this book. Every effort has been made to trace and contact copyright holders. If there are any inadvertent omissions we apologize to those concerned and undertake to include suitable acknowledgements in all future editions.*

Scripture quotations are taken from the following versions:

The *Contemporary English Version* © American Bible Society 1991, 1992, 1995. Used with permissions/Anglicizations © British & Foreign Bible Society 1997.

*The Holy Bible, New Century Version* © 1987, 1988, 1991 by Word Publishing. Anglicized version copyright © 1993 Nelson Word Ltd.

*The New Revised Standard Version of the Bible* copyright © 1989 by the Division of Christian Education of the National Council of Churches of the USA. All Rights Reserved.

Extract from *Patterns for Worship* (Church House Publishing, 1995) is copyright © The Central Board of Finance of the Church of England 1989, 1995; The Archbishops' Council 1999 and is reproduced by permission.

Extract from *Common Worship: Initiation Services* (Church House Publishing, 1998) is copyright © The Central Board of Finance of the Church of England, 1997, 1998; The Archbishops' Council 1999 and is reproduced by permission.

Extract from *Common Worship: Services and Prayers for the Church of England* (Church House Publishing, 2000) is copyright © The Archbishops' Council 2000 and is reproduced by permission.

Material in Supplementary handout 14 is adapted with permission from James Lawrence, *Lost for Words*, CPAS, 2002. For full details contact CPAS on (01926) 458456 or log on to www.cpas.org.uk.

'Spirit of the Living God' by Daniel Iverson is copyright © 1963 Birdwing Music/EMI Christian Publishing. Administered by Copycare, PO Box 77, Hailsham, BN27 3EF, UK. music@copycare.com. Used by permission.

# Preface

*Emmaus: the Way of Faith* was first published in 1996. Since then thousands of churches in Britain and around the world have used *Emmaus* to welcome people into the Christian faith and the life of the Church.

*Youth Emmaus* is offered in response to all those churches that enjoyed using the adult material, but wanted something similar for young people.

*Youth Emmaus* provides materials to help young people explore the basics of Christianity, as part of a process for accompanying them on the way of faith.

The adult material was designed in three stages:

- Contact – ideas for meeting people where they are;

- Nurture – a 15-session course for growing Christians;

- Growth – 13 short courses to help people go deeper into the basics of faith.

*Youth Emmaus* is a nurture course for young people. Although it follows the same format as the Nurture section of adult *Emmaus* the material has been specifically designed for the varied needs and experiences of young people today.

Many thousands of adults have come to faith through the *Emmaus* course. It is hoped that *Youth Emmaus* can do the same for many thousands of young people.

*Stephen Cottrell, Sue Mayfeld, Tim Sledge, Tony Washington*
*October 2002*

# Getting started

## Who is it for?

*Youth Emmaus* is aimed primarily at young people aged 11–16 who want to find out about the Christian faith.

- It is for young Christians who want to find out more and who may be preparing for baptism and confirmation.

- It is for fringe people.

- It is for those who want to explore.

## What is the format?

*Youth Emmaus* (like the adult Nurture course of *Emmaus*) comes in three parts:

- what Christians believe;

- how Christians grow;

- living the Christian life.

You can either invite people to the whole course, or split it into three sections, inviting them to one stage at a time.

Each session should last between 60 and 90 minutes. There is material for a 60-minute session, but it is best if this can happen in the context of a meeting that lasts 90 minutes. This way there is time for refreshments and extra time for some bits of the session if needed. It also means you can have a bit more fun with the Warming ups if you want to.

Between the different sections of the course we suggest that you pause and give the group a break, but also consider having a different sort of evening – either a social event or our suggested Hot Potatoes session. Perhaps questions will have arisen during some of the sessions which you haven't had time to answer as fully as you'd like. Keep a note of these as you go along. You could invite a 'special guest' to help you address some of these questions and issues (see further ideas in the 'Hot Potatoes' session, p. 68)).

For every session there are leaders' notes, followed by a handout for the group members. All the handouts are also available on the CD-ROM that comes with *Youth Emmaus*. The handouts can be photocopied for each group member or printed from the disk.

The leaders' notes carefully explain how the sessions are to be led, but *Youth Emmaus* is designed to be flexible. Group leaders are encouraged to plan the sessions in advance and to adapt the material according to their own instincts and experience, and according to the particular needs of their group.

In each session one activity is titled 'Mega byte' (see p. xix for key to the icons). This indicates its suitability for use with a group when going through a whole session might be inappropriate or impossible. In which case this activity, along with the 'Warming up' activity, gets you to the heart of the session. This might be particularly useful where most of the group don't yet come to church, or where you are using *Youth Emmaus* as part of an existing youth club, or where you are using it at lunchtime in schools and need much shorter sessions. It may also be useful if you have members of your group with learning difficulties.

The handouts are used in the sessions in different ways. Sometimes it will just be a take-home sheet. Sometimes there are activities to do on the sheet. Exactly how to use the handout is up to each group, and with some groups it will be best not to use them at all. In which case the material can work just as well without them.

## *The Emmaus Road experience*

For most people becoming a Christian is like a journey. The work of evangelism is therefore about helping people make the journey – listening, directing and patiently accompanying people on the way of faith.

The story of the Emmaus Road at the end of Luke's Gospel (Luke 24.13-35) gives us a wonderfully rich model for this ministry. It is the inspiration behind the *Emmaus* course.

Putting on an *Emmaus* group means sharing in that Christlike ministry of meeting people where they are and walking with them on their journey, sharing with them the good news of God's love.

Not all will come to faith in Christ. Neither can we control or predict how and when faith will be awakened in people. God himself is the evangelist: our job is to be good companions, faithfully witnessing to the gospel and showing Christ's love by the way we deal with people as well as by the words we say. This is the *Emmaus* way of evangelizing.

## Leading a group

It is best if there are two group leaders in each group. The leaders do not have to be clergy. It is good to have lay leaders: youth leaders and older members of your youth group (if you have any) will be a great help.

- Try to find an attractive and comfortable place to meet.

- Try to have some simple refreshments at each meeting.

- Try to make the sessions enjoyable.

Nothing very much will be achieved unless the young people enjoy coming to the sessions. The warm ups and activities in each session are there to help people get to know each other and have fun. They should not be left out unless something else is put in their place. They will help the group relax, and provide ways of helping the young people engage not just with each other but also with the material being explored.

Becoming a Christian involves much, much more than just learning about the faith. *Youth Emmaus* tries to help young people consider the implications of the faith for their own lives and grow in a living relationship with God, through the church. This is why praying together at each session is so vitally important.

Each session has ideas for prayer. But please supplement these with your own ideas, and encourage the young people to take a lead and to come up with their own ways of praying. At the back of the book in the Additional resources section there is a chapter on ways of building prayer into the sessions that is full of practical ideas and help.

If issues come up that you do not know how to deal with, or do not have time to deal with, make a note of them as you go along so that they can be dealt with at a special session.

Make sure the leaders' notes are looked at well in advance of the session. Often there will be objects and resources to assemble – so leave yourself enough time. Another book in the *Emmaus* series *Leading an Emmaus Group* will be very helpful. Although it was written about leading groups for adults, much of what it has to say is just as relevant for young people.

However, there are some specific issues that need to be dealt with very carefully.

## Child protection

Child protection has always been a matter of common sense and good practice. However, it is vital that every church has a child protection policy and someone who is responsible for implementing it. If in any doubt about these issues make sure you speak to someone in your church, or failing that seek advice elsewhere. All the denominations have someone at the diocesan, district or area level who can advise on this and provide you with any forms you will need.

The main areas you should be paying especial attention to are adult leaders and premises.

*Adult leaders*  All those working with young people need to be aware of and compliant with current child protection legislation. This is constantly changing so make sure your church is up to date and that all group leaders have been through a proper child protection checking procedure.

Groups should really have at least two leaders. If the group is mixed they should be male and female. If the group goes over 20 young people you should have a third leader.

Leaders should minimize the amount of time spent alone with a single young person.

*Premises*  You will not have to register your meeting place but it must be safe and well maintained. Things to look out for include:

- dangerous electrics, floor, stacked chairs etc. ;

- facilities: toilets, basins, a place to provide refreshments etc.;

- access to a phone;

- a fire/safety procedure, including an accident book;

- maintained fire extinguishers and first aid kit;

- public liability insurance. Is your activity covered?

Greater detail on child protection issues, including copies of forms you will need, can be obtained from your denomination or diocese.

## House rules

As part of the first session, it is helpful and useful to establish some house rules or ground rules for all the members. These will help create:

- trust

- confidence

- openness

- a relaxed environment.

Young people are reticent about sharing and offering information when talking about personal things like relationships and faith. Therefore, it is a good exercise to encourage the members to set their own ground rules. Take five minutes at the start of the first session to do this. Make sure that anything that is said in the room remains confidential, that people hear each other out, that all opinions are valued.

A set of house rules might look something like this:

- Make sure everyone has their say, if they want.

- Never interrupt when someone else is talking.

- All opinions are valid.

- Don't laugh at others.

- Don't gossip outside the room about what went on in the group.

## *Soul friends – companions on the way*

The Emmaus Road in Luke's Gospel is a story of an accompanied journey – Jesus walks alongside Cleopas and his companion. At first Jesus just listens and lets them set the agenda and lead. But later on he becomes the guide and eventually they are turned around by their encounter with Jesus.

*Youth Emmaus* also seeks to accompany young people on a journey of discovery. It is hoped that young people's lives will be turned around and refocused as they encounter the living Christ in the fellowship of his Church.

One of the ways of expressing this companionship on the way of faith is through appointing 'soul friends' for the young people in the group. These could be adult members of the congregation who simply pray for the young people, or who get involved with helping to run the groups. Or it could be other young people who are already members of the church.

The basic principle is that those who are already walking in the way of Christ accompany those exploring faith.

The role of these companions is to:

- pray for the young people in the group;

- attend and join in the sessions (if this seems appropriate for your group);

- be a point of contact for them when they come to church.

But there is much more that can be done if people are enthusiastic and it seems appropriate, such as buying a Bible for a group member or sending encouraging emails.

Some groups have a soul friend for each group member. In most cases it is probably enough to have a few people taking on this role for the whole group.

Those taking on this ministry need to be prepared. But this shouldn't take long. It will probably be sufficient to get them together before the group starts meeting and explain how they will join in the sessions, their responsibility to pray for the young people and their ministry of welcome and hospitality so that as the young people grow in faith they will have people in the church whom they know and can turn to
if they want to.

Having soul friends as part of the *Emmaus* process

- expresses more clearly what Jesus was doing on the Emmaus Road;

- models the community of the church for each *Emmaus* group;

- helps young people feel part of the wider church community.

It is to be recommended!

## Getting young people to come on *Youth Emmaus*

If your church already has a group of young people meeting regularly, or a group of young people wanting to explore the Christian faith or be confirmed, then starting *Youth Emmaus* will be quite straightforward. Even so you need to find out about the young people. *Youth Emmaus* always works best when it is part of a process of accompanying and befriending young people and helping them on their journey through life. If you want to use the course to reach out or to make contact with young people then a bit more work is required.

*Youth Emmaus* won't work very well in a vacuum. If yours is one of those churches where you are wondering where all the young people have got to, then you need to begin by developing relationships with young people before you will be able to do anything else.

Many churches have a number of children of church members who don't come to church any more. Try to find out why. Offer them a place to meet and some activities to plan and take part in. Often the best way to get a course like *Youth Emmaus* started is simply to get a group of young people together and do things with them that they find interesting or enjoying. Then the course itself can be introduced, perhaps by starting with the 'Mega byte' and 'Warming up' activities so you are not doing too much too soon.

Perhaps you have a local Church or state secondary school. Are there Christian staff who would appreciate support in offering *Youth Emmaus* to a Christian Union or after-school club? At least one of the churches piloting *Youth Emmaus* began it as a lunchtime group in school.

Perhaps you are in contact with a local youth organization. If church members are involved in such groups then relationships can be built up with young people that may provide openings for running *Youth Emmaus*.

The most important thing, once you have identified some young people, is to start where they are. What are their social and spiritual needs? What are their backgrounds and knowledge? How can you, the local church, serve this group? Teenagers are wary of being targeted and made the object of a campaign. You will only reach them with genuine, non-judgemental friendship. If your interest in them is going to fizzle out after *Youth Emmaus* is over, don't even start it. Youth work is a long-term enterprise. *Youth Emmaus* is a short-term resource to help young people on the way of faith, but one that has proved useful to get churches started again in this crucial and often neglected ministry, and to help them do a better job when it comes to exploring issues of faith.

## *Celebrations on the way*

In the Additional resources section at the back of the book there are three liturgies that can be used to enhance the process of *Youth Emmaus* and celebrate the journey to faith that young people are travelling.

### *Marking the start of the Emmaus journey*

- for those beginning *Youth Emmaus*.

### *A liturgy of commitment*

- for those who have made a decision to follow Christ and are looking forward to baptism and/or confirmation or some other public declaration of faith.

### *A celebration of the faith of young people*

- a liturgy to use at the end of *Youth Emmaus* for the young people to design and lead themselves.

These services enrich the whole process.

## Youth culture

The most important thing you'll need to remember about your group is that they are all individuals with their own likes and dislikes, strengths and weaknesses, problems and joys. It is always helpful to start with this thought or there is a danger of stereotyping the young people who will join your group.

The term 'youth culture', however, suggests that young people do have certain things in common. They are in a transition between childhood and adulthood. Their bodies are changing, their minds are expanding and their relationships are becoming more complex. At this stage of vulnerability in their lives young people can really value a relationship with a non-judging adult – although there might be times when this isn't apparent!

Young people are also under lots of pressure from their peers, worrying about what others think. For these reasons it is important that *Youth Emmaus* is well led so that each person can relax and get the most from it. Setting house rules will help eliminate behaviour that excludes or ridicules people. Respecting people's beliefs and opinions even when we don't agree is also important. As a leader it is not your job to make the group believe what you do but to help them access the facts and attitudes that enable them to make up their own minds.

## Postmodern culture

The cultural changes that have taken place over the past 20 or so years have made it harder for the Christian message to be heard and understood. The world that young people are growing up into is a very different place to the one that most adults experienced when they were growing up.

The postmodern mindset is characterized by a rejection of absolutes and the institutions that have been built upon them. Religious faith, even the concepts of 'right' and 'wrong', have become casualties.

For young people nowadays the questions 'does it work?' and 'how does it feel?' are likely to be more important than 'is it true?' It is the leaders' job to live out or demonstrate what it means to be a Christian.

Young people influenced by postmodernity may well already have a belief system that is based purely on what they or their friends think without any reference to an organized religion. It may be a 'pick and mix' of beliefs from all over the place. They may never have learnt what Christians believe in an engaging way. Here is your chance.

### *Young and old together*

*Youth Emmaus* can also be run with a group made up of people of different ages. Some churches will find that they have a group of people wanting to explore the Christian faith and one will be an older person, and one a single mum with two small children, and then you will have a couple of teenagers.

The adult Nurture course and *Youth Emmaus* follow each other quite closely, and at the back of this book in the Additional resources section there is a chapter with activities to be used when small children might be present in the group, thus making it possible to run *Emmaus* as a group for all ages.

## And just before you begin . . .

Get to know the parents of the children. Find out if any of them have any difficulties reading. Ask if there is anything else that it would be helpful to know so as to avoid embarrassments.

You are leading the group. Hopefully there will be no need for discipline, but if there is, the members need to know that you are in charge! Your set of house rules will be useful to refer to here.

Above all, love these young people, and create an environment where they can know your love and love one another! At a time of crucial identity formation in their lives they have the opportunity, through *Youth Emmaus*, to learn about and meet their creator and Lord. Some simply may not be ready for this and they all have the freedom not to take up the offer. Do all you can to create a safe environment where Christian faith can be encountered and explored. During this course, more than anything else, the group members will learn from you. You will be modelling for them what being a Christian is actually like. If you show them proper and appropriate love and concern, and if you are able to demonstrate to them your love for God and your commitment to the Christian life, then you will have been a good companion to them on the way of faith. And this is what *Youth Emmaus* is all about. If in doubt, don't put your trust in the material (helpful though we hope it is) but in the God who calls and who accompanies, and who gives us a share in his ministry of love to the world.

# Key to icons used in the leaders' notes and members' handouts

## home page

A brief summary of what the session is all about.

## interfacing

The prayer activity.

## warming up

Games and activities to get you started.

## backing up

A reminder for leaders of what the session is all about.

## logging on

Reflecting on the previous week's session and leading into this one.

## processing

Something for the young people to think about as a result of the session.

## byte

Activity or discussion to explore the theme of the session.

## do something about it

Something for the young people to do as a result of the session.

## mega byte

The main activity for the session and the one to focus in on if you want to run a shorter session or if the young people are just beginning to explore issues of faith.

## coming soon

Looking forward to the next session.

Part 1

# what christians believe

# Knowing god 1 — is there anyone out there?

## home page

In this first session we ask the basic question 'Is there a God?' and explore the evidence for God's existence in the natural world and in ourselves. As this is the first session of *Youth Emmaus* this unit also aims to help group members to feel comfortable with the course and with each other.

**For this session you will need:**
* a collection of natural objects – flowers, leaves, shells, stones, feathers, pine cones, etc;
* slides and projector (if available);
* blank paper and pens;
* a soft ball (juggling balls are ideal), if you are using 'Warming up's 1 or 2.

## warming up

Choose *one* of the three 'getting to know you' 'Warming up' activities.

### 1. Name ball
Hand a soft ball (a juggling ball is ideal) around the circle. Each person says their name as they pass the ball to the next person. Now ask the young people to throw the ball randomly to each other saying their own name and the name of the person they are throwing to so that a rhythmic pattern develops; e.g. 'Jamie–Katie' (Jamie throws to Katie), 'Katie–Simon' (Katie throws to Simon), etc. Keep playing until everyone has been included.

### 2. Food ball
This is the same as above, only instead of saying their names as they throw the ball the young people say their favourite food; e.g. 'chicken tikka–pizza', 'pizza–chocolate ice cream', etc.

### 3. I went to Emmaus . . .
Sit in a circle. The leader begins by saying ' I went to Emmaus and I took . . .', filling the blank with an object that defines his or her character; e.g. my bed, a chocolate bar, purple nail varnish, a football. The next person in the circle says the same but adds an object of his or her choice to the object already suggested; e.g. 'I went to Emmaus and I took my bed and my favourite CD . . .' As the list gets longer the young people have to work hard to remember what object defined each person!

## logging on

Welcome the young people to the course and explain the format sessions will take. It is a good idea to establish some ground rules for the group at this point (see p. xiv)

Explain that this first session asks the question 'Is there anyone out there?' Encourage the young people to be honest about their own beliefs.

# knowing god 1—is there anyone out there?

## True or false

byte

Do a short True or False quiz as a group. Make up ten questions about things like music, sport and the natural world. (Choose questions suitable to your group.) Get group members to indicate silently 'true' (thumbs up) or 'false' (thumbs down) after each statement.

After the quiz ask the question, *'God exists – True or false?'*

## Wonderful world

mega byte

Lay out the selection of natural objects and invite the young people to choose one and hold it. Invite them to look very closely at it and think about its design.

Ask them each to say something they notice about their object.

Alternatively, if you have the facilities (and the slides), show slides of the natural world – sunsets, waterfalls, mountains, space, plants or wildlife. Play a piece of music to accompany the pictures.

Ask the group what amazes them most about the natural world. (You could write their answers on a flipchart or whiteboard.)

## Wonderful me!

byte

If the members of your group don't know each other prior to the start of the course use this:

### All about you

Make up a simple questionnaire with fanzine-type questions such as 'What's your favourite food/colour/band/chocolate bar?' 'What's your best place ever?' and 'What's your most embarrassing moment?' Invite group members to use the questionnaire to interview a partner. They could then introduce their partner to the rest of the group. Get them to focus on what makes each person unique and special.

If your group already know each other do the following:

### Positives

Sellotape a blank sheet of paper to each person's back. Give out pens. Put on some loud music (choose a current chart song – preferably a song about self and identity). Invite the group to move about, writing positive things on each others' backs – suggest things like what the person is good at, what their mates think of them and what makes them distinctive.

After a few minutes ask the young people to remove their paper and read what others have written about them. Ask each person to read aloud one nice thing someone wrote about them.

*continued >*

# knowing god 1—is there anyone out there?

## byte

*continued >*

Now ask:

- Where do our special qualities and our uniqueness come from?

- Where did we get our instinctive sense of right and wrong?

- Why do we have an urge to worship someone or something?

Encourage the group to think about these questions and to discuss them if appropriate.

## interfacing

Give out blank sheets of paper. Ask the young people to write down *one word* that best describes God. Put the pieces of paper face down in the middle, shuffle them and ask the group each to collect one piece. Take turns to say 'God is …' and then to add the word on the paper. When all the group have read out their words the group leader says a simple prayer.

Read the extract from Psalm 8 together slowly (it's printed on the members' handout). If possible do this outdoors in a garden, or park, or better still on top of a hill!

## backing up

Whether or not God exists is a vital question to ask. The answer could affect your whole life. If there is a God, life takes on an extra dimension – there is more to life than what we see and there is purpose and design in the natural world. If there is a God then we are made in the image of a creator and not just random accidents or collections of molecules.

If there is no God there is no divine purpose and plan and people have to find meaning and purpose from other things.

Christians believe that there is plenty of evidence for God's existence in nature and in humankind. But we all have to decide for ourselves: *God exists – True or false?*

## coming soon

Encourage the young people to consider what they are going to pray about, think about and do as a result of this week's session.

Suggest that they take home their list of positives (if you used this activity) and read it daily.

| Suggested timings: | |
| --- | --- |
| Warming up | 10 mins |
| Logging on | 5 mins |
| Byte: True or false quiz | 5 mins |
| Megabyte: Wonderful world | 10 mins |
| Byte: Wonderful me! | 15 mins |
| Interfacing | 10 mins |
| Backing up/Coming soon | 5 mins |

# Knowing God 1 — is there anyone out there?

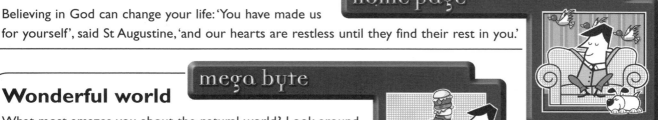

**home page**

Believing in God can change your life: 'You have made us for yourself', said St Augustine, 'and our hearts are restless until they find their rest in you.'

**mega byte**

## Wonderful world

What most amazes you about the natural world? Look around you this week at plants, trees, the weather, your pets – even your own face in the mirror!

How did it all get there? Was it an accident or did someone design it?

**byte**

## Wonderful me!

Write down the thing you most like about yourself.

Humans are amazing. They have the capacity

- to love and be loved;
- to laugh and to act generously;
- to create things;
- to feel pain and to be hurt;
- to distinguish right from wrong;
- to make choices.

*To be human is to be made in the likeness or image of God.*

This psalm celebrates the place of human beings in creation:

I often think of the heavens your hands have made,
and of the moon and stars you put in place.
Then I ask, 'Why do you care about us humans?
Why are you concerned for us weaklings?'
You made us a little lower than you yourself,
and you have crowned us with glory and honour.

You let us rule everything your hands have made.
And you put all of it under our power –
the sheep and the cattle, and every wild animal,
the birds in the sky, the fish in the sea,
and all ocean creatures.
Our Lord and Ruler,
Your name is wonderful everywhere on earth!

Psalm 8.3-9 CEV

>

# knowing god 1 — is there anyone out there?

## interfacing

Dear God,
Thank you for the beauty and wonder of the world.
Help me to recognize you in your creation.
Amen.

Thank God for the places, things and people you see every day.

Thank him for his wonderful world.

## processing

Have you ever wondered:

- Why did God make me?
- What is my life for?

Think about it!

## do something about it

Make a point of noticing creation more, perhaps on your way to school.

You could even make a collection of natural things like shells, leaves or conkers in your bedroom.

## coming soon

Next week: Your secret life with God – ways to know God personally.

# knowing god 2 — your secret life with god

home page

We can know God for ourselves. In this session we explore what God is like and consider our own relationship with him.

## warming up

### Guess the object

Hide a collection of household objects (ten or so, e.g. fruit, stapler, cuddly toy, pine cone) inside socks – one sock per object (tie the top of the sock to conceal what is hidden). Hand round the socks and invite group members to identify the objects using sense of touch and imagination only. You could award points for correct guesses.

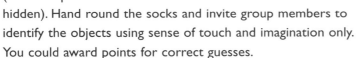

## logging on

Ask the group what they remember from last week and if they have any questions or things to say arising from Session 1.

Explain that last week we looked at whether God was real. This week we look more closely at what God is like and how we can know him personally.

Ask the young people how they identified the objects in the socks. How can we identify and recognize God? We can't see God or reach out and touch him but we can glimpse him in lots of different ways – in a beautiful piece of music, in the lives of other Christians, as we pray, as we experience someone's care for us, or in the Bible.

**You will need:**

* a range of household objects hidden in individual socks! (See instructions for 'Warming up');
* large sheets of paper or strips of white wallpaper (enough for one each) and chunky marker pens (one each);
* nightlight candles and matches;
* copies of the Sarum Primer, if used (see 'Interfacing' section);
* a poster of Rembrandt's painting *Return of the Prodigal Son* (available from St Paul Multimedia, 199 Kensington High Street, London W8 6BA Tel: 020 7937 9591 Fax: 020 7937 9910).

# knowing god 2— your secret life with god

## Life Path

Give each group member a large piece of paper and invite them to draw a winding path on it. Ask them to write 'Born' at one end of the path and 'Now' at the other. Then invite them to write (or draw in diagram form) significant events along the path, such as first steps, first day at school, best holiday, learnt to ride a bike, first kiss, etc. Encourage them to include significant events in their Christian journey too such as baptism, beginning to go to church, starting *Youth Emmaus*, first starting to think about God. (You could do a Life Path yourself and show it to the group to give them the idea.)

Invite the young people to share their Life Path with the rest of the group if they feel comfortable doing so.

## Father and Son

Read the story of the prodigal son, Luke 15.11-24. If possible look at a poster of Rembrandt's painting *Return of the Prodigal Son* as you listen to the story.

Ask the group what *one word* describes for them what the father in the story is like. (Write words on a flipchart or whiteboard.)

Now ask the group to picture themselves as the lost son in the story. Where are they in relation to God *at this moment* in their lives?

● Look at the list of statements on the handout and tick one of the boxes.

● Imagine one end of your meeting room represents the father's house and the other end represents the pigsty in a far country. Invite group members to go and stand at the place in the room that best describes where they currently are.

## Spot the difference

What difference does knowing God make?

Look at the three examples given on the handout. Invite the young people to talk in pairs or small groups about which, if any, of these three images they can relate to. This is an opportunity for the young people to talk about their own experience of God.

For some, perhaps those who have grown up in a Christian home, it will be hard to describe life with God if they cannot remember a time without him.

*continued >*

# knowing god 2 — your secret life with god

## byte

*continued >*

Others may never have considered this and will not understand the question.

Use the opportunity to make the distinction between merely knowing about God and actually knowing him.

Testimony is a powerful thing. It is better to generate discussion about the real life experiences of the young people themselves, however poorly they may be understood or expressed, than to go through theories of what knowing God might be like.

## interfacing

- Give each group member a lighted candle and encourage them all to be very still.

- Read Psalm 46.10: 'Be still and know that I am God.'

- Say a prayer inviting God to make himself known to each member of the group during the weeks of the course, like a light going on in the dark.

- You could photocopy the Sarum Primer 'God be in my head' from the Prayer Helpsheet (p. 123) and read it together.

## backing up

We may not be able to reach out and touch God but we can know him in a real and personal way. Getting to know God is a lifelong journey. Many things help us to get to know God – prayer, worship, Holy Communion, the Bible, being with other Christians, loving and serving those around us. Many of these things will be looked at more closely later in the course.

Most of all, we get to know God through Jesus – but more of that next week.

## coming soon

Encourage the group to use the suggestions for praying, thinking and action on the handout.

**Suggested timings:**

| | |
|---|---|
| Warming up | 5 mins |
| Logging on and feedback | 5 mins |
| Byte: Life Path | 15 mins |
| Megabyte: Father and son | 15 mins |
| Byte: Spot the difference | 10 mins |
| Interfacing | 5 mins |
| Backing up/Coming soon | 5 mins |

# Knowing God 2 — your secret life with God

## home page

God wants us to get to know him! This is the great adventure of the Christian life.

## byte

### Life Path

- What are the most significant events in your life so far?

- What things have been important in your journey towards God?

- Can you think of a time when you have been aware of God in your life?

## mega byte

### Father and Son

Jesus told a story about a father with two sons. One son took his half of his father's wealth and went away to a far country. There he wasted the money until he was broke and hungry. After a spell feeding someone else's pigs he decided to go home and beg for a job as one of his father's paid workers. He must have feared his father's anger as he turned for home. But the father was so glad to see his lost son returning that he ran to him and hugged him tight. Welcoming his son back home, the father threw a huge party to celebrate his return.

Read the story again in Luke 15.11-24. What is the father in the story like?

Jesus told this story to show us what God is like.

Imagine yourself as the son. Which stage in the story do you feel you have reached?

Tick the statement that best describes where *you* are in relation to God now, at this moment.

| | |
|---|---|
| Running away | ○ |
| Having a good time in the far-off land | ○ |
| Feeling empty and lost in the far-off land | ○ |
| Turning round to come back | ○ |
| On your way home | ○ |
| In the arms of the father | ○ |
| Back in the heart of the family | ○ |

> |

# knowing god 2— your secret life with god

## Spot the difference

Christians have described the difference that God makes to their lives in a number of ways.

**The 'God-shaped hole'.** Some people have described not knowing God as like having a gap in their lives. It feels as if something is missing. You try to fill the hole with all sorts of good (and bad) things but in the end nothing will satisfy you except God.

**Glorious technicolour.** Others have described discovering God as like the difference between black-and-white TV and colour. The picture is the same in black and white but everything is richer and more interesting in colour. Life with God is (in many ways) the same as before but now it is enriched and enhanced.

**Darkness and light.** The Bible often speaks of people being in darkness without God. Getting to know him is like switching on the light – or like the breaking of the dawn.

Which of these ideas makes the most sense to *you*?

## interfacing

Thank God that, like the father in the story, he opens his arms to welcome you.

Ask God to make himself known to you more and more.

## processing

What are the things that help you to 'see' God?

## do something about it

Ask an older person in your church what difference knowing God makes to them?

## coming soon

Next week: The life and ministry of Jesus.

# 3
# Jesus — his life and ministry

## home page

We can get to know God through the world that God has made. We can get to know God through reflecting on our experiences of life. We can get to know God through the Bible, the church, through prayer and through worship. But for Christians all this makes little sense without Jesus. Jesus is God's way of getting to know God. This session is about how God has revealed himself in Jesus.

**For this session you will need:**

* pictures of Jesus. Gather your own, or use the CMS/USPG resource *The Christ We Share*, a collection of images of Jesus from all around the world;
* biblical texts about Jesus. Photocopy and cut up the supplementary handout on pp. 17–18;
* blank postcards, and coloured pencils, pens, pastels or paints;
* list of ten famous people (dead or alive ) for 'Warming up'.

## warming up

### Who am I?

Play the 20 questions Boticelli game. Someone in the group chooses a famous person, living or dead and then answers questions such as 'Are you alive?', 'Are you a man?', 'Are you a footballer?' 'Do you have a famous wife?' with Yes or No answers. The group have 20 questions to guess the mystery person's identity. (It might be a good idea to prepare a list of possible people – sportspeople, popstars, politicians, etc. – in advance, in case your group are short on ideas.)

## logging on

Explain that this session is about Jesus and the ways in which he shows us what God is like. Ask the group how much they can remember about last week's session. Invite them to talk (either as a whole group or in pairs) about the things they have been praying about, thinking about and putting into practice as a result of last week's session. Be ready to contribute some of your own (brief!) reflections.

**mega byte**

## Picture this!

Collect as many pictures and images of Jesus as you can. Spread them out on the floor. Invite the young people to choose the picture that most speaks to them about who they think Jesus is, and what is important about him. Encourage them to talk about the picture they have chosen with each other in twos or threes or as a whole group.

**byte**

## Window into God

Jesus is a window into God. He shows us what God is like — what his priorities are, how he deals with people, what he feels about the world.

Photocopy the sheet of six short gospel passages from the supplementary handout. Cut them up and place them in a pot. Get the young people, one at a time, to take a piece of paper out of the pot and read it. (If you have young people in your group who struggle with literacy make sure you do this in pairs, or ask for volunteer readers.) For each Bible reading ask the question, 'What does this passage tell us about God?' Either discuss this as a whole group, or get the young people to discuss first in pairs and then offer their conclusions to the whole group.

*With some of the passages ask the group other questions to provoke them to think creatively about who Jesus is.*

**byte**

## 'Who do you say I am?'

Read Matthew 16.13-16 (this passage is printed on the handout).

This is the vital question that every human being must face — who is Jesus of Nazareth?

- Is he a misguided fool?

- Is he a great teacher and philosopher?

- Is he a wonder worker?

- Is he God come down to earth?

*continued >*

# Jesus — his life and ministry

## byte

*continued >*

No one can answer this question for you. The Christian faith proclaims that God is in Jesus. In Jesus our life is united with the life of God. At his birth Jesus came and shared our human life. When he died on the cross he shared our human death. When he rose again he carried our human life home to God, and opened the way for people to have life with God. God shares our life on earth, so that we can share his life in heaven.

But what do *you* think?

Give all the group members a blank postcard. On one side they write a one-line answer to Jesus' question, 'Who do you say I am?' On the other side they draw their own picture of Jesus.

## interfacing

- Use the postcard answers as a short act of worship. The group leader asks the question, 'Who do you say I am?', and each group member reads the response on their card.

- Use the litany on the supplementary handout. Photocopy it so everyone can have a copy.

## backing up

Jesus is God's way to God. We can catch glimpses of God in creation and in our own experience. Many human beings have a sense of God (or at least try to make sense of life) and most cultures have religions that reach out to God. But only Christianity says that God has come looking for us! Jesus is God finding us and loving us: God in human flesh showing us what God is like. The Bible gives us a faithful record of what the very first Christians believed and experienced, and through the Bible we can find out about Jesus and begin to come to our own conclusions.

## coming soon

Encourage the young people to think about what they are going to pray about, think about and do as a result of this week's session.

**Suggested timings:**

| | |
|---|---|
| Warming up | 10 mins |
| Logging on and feedback | 5 mins |
| Megabyte: Picture this! | 10 mins |
| Byte: Window into God | 15 mins |
| Byte: 'Who do you say I am?' | 10 mins |
| Interfacing | 5 mins |
| Backing up/Coming soon | 5 mins |

# jesus — his life and ministry

## home page

Jesus is God's way of getting to know God. Through Jesus, God shows us what he is like.

## mega byte

### Picture this!

Many Christians use pictures of Jesus – sometimes called icons – to help them pray. How do you picture Jesus?

## byte

## Window into God

Jesus shows us what God is like. In the Gospels we see Jesus doing many things – eating with people, healing the sick, telling stories, teaching about God, performing miracles, being born, dying and rising again.

Look at the list below and circle the word you think best describes Jesus.

| | |
|---|---|
| **Teacher** | **Human** |
| **Healer** | **Saviour** |
| **Miracle worker** | **Friend** |
| **Storyteller** | **Leader** |

## byte

## Who is Jesus?

When Jesus and his disciples were near to the town of Caesarea Philippi, he asked them, 'What do people say about the Son of Man?'

> **The disciples answered, 'Some people say you are John the Baptist, or perhaps Elijah or Jeremiah or some other prophet.'**
> **Then Jesus asked them, 'But who do you say I am?'**
> **Simon Peter spoke up, 'You are the Messiah, the Son of the living God.'**

*Matthew 16.13-16 CEV*

*continued >*

# jesus — his life and ministry

## byte

*continued >*

'Who do you say that I am?' This is the vital question that every human being must face – who is Jesus of Nazareth?

- Is he a misguided fool?
- Is he a great teacher and philosopher?
- Is he a wonder worker?
- Is he God come down to earth?

No one can answer this question for you.

The Christian faith proclaims that God is revealed to us in Jesus. Jesus shares our human life. On the cross he shares our human death. By rising again he opens the way for us to have life with God. God shares our life on earth, so that we can share his life in heaven.

But what do *you* think?

## interfacing

Find (or make) a picture of Jesus and use it as a focus for your prayers. Speak to Jesus as you would a close friend. Tell him what is on your mind. Ask him to help you believe.

## processing

Why did God send Jesus into the world? It was a risky thing to do . . .

## do something about it

Read the story of Jesus' death and resurrection in Luke's Gospel (Luke 23.1 – 24.12).

## coming soon

Next week: The death and resurrection of Jesus.

# jesus — his life and ministry

Then the angel told Mary, 'Don't be afraid! God is pleased with you, and you will have a son. His name will be Jesus. He will be great and will be called the Son of God Most High. The Lord God will make him king, as his ancestor David was.'

*Luke 1.30-32 CEV*

Jesus went back to Nazareth, where he had been brought up, and as usual he went to the meeting place on the Sabbath. When he stood up to read from the Scriptures, he was given the book of Isaiah the prophet. He opened it and read,

'The Lord's Spirit has come to me, because he has chosen me to tell the good news to the poor. The Lord has sent me to announce freedom for prisoners, to give sight to the blind, to free everyone who suffers, and to say "This is the year the Lord has chosen." '

*Luke 4.16-19 CEV*

Jesus came to a town where there was a man who had leprosy. When the man saw Jesus, he knelt down on the ground in front of Jesus and begged, 'Lord, you have the power to make me well, if only you wanted to.'

Jesus put his hand on him and said, 'I want to! Now you are well.' At once the man's leprosy disappeared.

*Luke 5.12-13 CEV*

Jesus said, 'Treat others just as you want to be treated.'

*Luke 6.31 CEV*

# jesus — his life and ministry

Jesus said, 'Why do you keep on saying that I am your Lord, when you refuse to do what I say? Anyone who comes and listens to me and obeys me is like someone who dug down deep and built a house on solid rock. When the flood came and the river rushed against the house, it was built so well that it didn't even shake. But anyone who hears what I say and doesn't obey me is like someone whose house wasn't built on solid rock. As soon as the river rushed against that house, it was smashed to pieces!'

*Luke 6.46-9 CEV*

One day, Jesus and his disciples got into a boat, and he said, 'Lets cross the lake.' They started out, and while they were sailing across, he went to sleep.

Suddenly a storm struck the lake, and the boat started sinking. They were in danger. So they went to Jesus and woke him up, 'Master, Master! We are about to drown!'

Jesus got up and ordered the wind and waves to stop. They obeyed, and everything was calm. Then Jesus asked the disciples, 'Don't you have any faith?' But they were frightened and amazed. They said to each other, 'Who is this? He can give orders to the wind and the waves and they obey him!'

*Luke 8.22-5 CEV*

## A Litany

We pray to Jesus who is present with us to
  eternity, saying,

Jesus, Lord of life:

**in your mercy, hear us.**


Jesus, light of the world,

bring the light and peace of your gospel

to the nations …

Jesus, Lord of life:

**in your mercy, hear us.**


Jesus, bread of life,

give food to the hungry …

and nourish us all with your word.

Jesus, Lord of life:

**in your mercy, hear us.**


Jesus our way, our truth, our life,

be with us all who follow you in the way …

deepen our appreciation of your truth,

and fill us with your life.

Jesus, Lord of life:

**in your mercy, hear us.**


Jesus, Good Shepherd who gave your life for
  the sheep,

recover the straggler, bind up the injured,

strengthen the sick

and lead the healthy and strong to play.

Jesus, Lord of life:

**in your mercy, hear us.**


Jesus, the resurrection and the life,

we give you thanks

for all who have lived and believed in you …

raise us with them to eternal life.

Jesus, Lord of life:

**in your mercy, hear us,
accept our prayers, and be with us
always. Amen.**


From *Patterns for Worship,*
Church House Publishing, 1995, pp. 72–3.

# Jesus — his death and resurrection

home page

The death and resurrection of Jesus are the very heart of the Christian faith. Without the resurrection, Jesus is just another good man who said and did good things. The resurrection shows us he is God's son, the one who is victorious over sin and death. Without his death on the cross, Jesus isn't fully human. His death shows us how much God shares in and wants to transform human life.

**For this session you will need:**

* some chocolate biscuits;
* a video of the life of Jesus (*Miracle Maker* or *Jesus of Nazareth*);
* a photocopy of the supplementary handout cut into six strips and put in a pot or basket;
* two crosses — one a crucifix and one an empty cross. (If you haven't got these you could use pictures of crosses. The CMS pack *Across the World* is an excellent resource.)

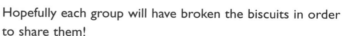

## Chocolate biscuits

Divide into groups of three. Give each group *two* chocolate biscuits and ask them to share them out. Before they eat the biscuits the groups show each other how they have done the sharing.

Hopefully each group will have broken the biscuits in order to share them!

Introduce the idea of how things often have to be broken before they can be shared. Show the group a few other examples (a Christmas cracker, a walnut, an egg, bread, a satsuma, and whatever else you can think of).

logging on

Invite everyone to share with each other, either in pairs or as a whole group, things they have been thinking about since the last session. Did they read the story of Jesus' death and resurrection? What did they make of it? Why *did* God send Jesus into the world?

Explain that this session looks at why Jesus died and rose again and asks, 'What does it all mean?'

# jesus — his death and resurrection

## mega byte

### Video

Show a video of Jesus' death and resurrection.

If your group is quite young use *Miracle Maker* (5-minute extract 72 minutes into the film).

If they are a bit older use *Jesus of Nazareth* (18-minute extract 1 hour 44 minutes into the second video of the 270-minute two-video film version).

(If for some reason you are unable to show a video, the story can be read out, perhaps using different voices for different parts. *The Dramatised Bible* (Marshall Pickering, 1989) has dramatized versions of the gospel story.)

After watching your chosen clip give the group time to react to it and to discuss their responses. Don't underestimate how moved or upset they may be. (*Jesus of Nazareth* is a particularly harrowing reconstruction of the crucifixion.)

## byte

### Jerusalem TV

- Split the young people into at least two groups (an ideal group size would be 4–5).

- Tell them they are working for Jerusalem TV. It is Easter Sunday. They have to produce a short piece for the evening news. It should describe the events of the past three days and include interviews with leading characters in the story.

- Encourage them to focus on *why* Jesus died and rose again and to ask the question, 'What does it all mean?'

- Give the groups time to plan and practise their pieces and then watch them.

# Jesus — his death and resurrection

## byte

### Cross examined

This activity looks more closely at the meaning of the cross and the resurrection.

- Sit in a circle.

- Put the six statements photocopied from the supplementary handout into a pot in the middle of the circle.

- Hand round the two crosses (or the pictures of a crucifix and empty cross). Invite the young people to handle them and to comment on them and their reactions to them.

- Now put the crosses in the middle of the circle.

- Ask six volunteers to take pieces of paper from the pot and read what is on them to the group. Then lay them alongside the crosses.

- Ask the group members which of the six statements means most to them, and why.

## interfacing

Remain in the circle with the crosses in the middle. Listen to a reflective piece of music about the cross, either a worship song, or something more traditional such as something from St John Passion by Bach. Say together the prayer on the handout.

## backing up

The death and resurrection of Jesus show how God shares our life, loves us, forgives us and has a purpose for our lives. We need to respond to what God has done, share it with others and live it each day.

## coming soon

Encourage the young people to pray, think and do as outlined on the handout.

### Suggested timings:

| | |
|---|---|
| Warming up | 5 mins |
| Logging on and feedback | 3 mins |
| Megabyte: Video | 15 mins |
| Byte: Jerusalem TV | 20 mins |
| Byte: Cross examined | 10 mins |
| Interfacing | 5 mins |
| Backing up/Coming soon | 2 mins |

# Jesus — his death and resurrection

## home page

The death and resurrection of Jesus show how God shares our life, loves us, forgives us and has a purpose for our lives.

## mega byte

### God's rescue mission

- God made us and loves us.

- We were made to know God and have a close relationship with him. But we turned away. We followed our own paths. We are cut off from God by all the things we think and say and do that separate us from him – our pride, our selfishness, our sins.

- Our hearts are restless, and without God we have no hope of heaven.

- But God sent Jesus to save us from our sins and their effects.

- The name Jesus means 'Saviour'. Jesus died so that we can enjoy a new relationship with God.

- His resurrection is the proof that all God's promises are true.

## Check out the evidence for the resurrection ...

That Jesus rose from the dead may seem a little hard to believe. After all, it isn't exactly an everyday occurrence! But what about:

- **The empty tomb.** Despite the fact the tomb was guarded, the stone was rolled away. If Jesus didn't rise from the dead, where did his body go? If the authorities had taken it (and why should they?) they would have produced it when claims about the resurrection were made later.

- **The witnesses.** More than 500 people claimed to have seen Jesus alive. Their encounters changed their lives and they were prepared to die for their belief. The witnesses not only saw him – they talked with him, walked with him, learnt from him, ate with him and touched him.

*continued >*

# Jesus — his death and resurrection

*continued >*

## mega byte

- **The Church began.** After the cross the disciples were demoralized and defeated. They were afraid of what might happen to them. They denied that they even knew Jesus. Only a few days later they were risking their lives to proclaim Jesus as the Saviour. Their witness turned the world upside down. What event (other than the resurrection) could have so transformed them? Would you travel to the ends of the earth to spread a message you had made up? Would you die for something you had imagined?

- **The testimony of Christians.** For 2,000 years, in every culture, men and women have claimed that we can know Jesus for ourselves. This is happening today in our country, in our town, in our church.

## interfacing

Use this prayer this week:

**Eternal God, in whom is all our hope
in life, in death, and to all eternity:
grant that, rejoicing in the eternal life
which is ours in Christ,
we may face whatever the future holds in
store for us calm and unafraid,
always confident that neither death nor life
can part us from your love in Jesus Christ
our Lord.**

**Amen.**

## processing

Read the section about God's Rescue Mission on this sheet, again.

Does it make sense?

## do something about it

Make your own cross. You could use wood, twigs bound together with thread, pipe cleaners, clay or card and paint. Put it somewhere where it will remind you of Jesus' death and resurrection.

## coming soon

Next week:
The Holy Spirit.

# jesus — his death and resurrection

The cross shows us that **God shares everything about being human, including suffering and death.**

**The cross shows us that God loves us – Jesus lays down his life for his friends.** Imagine you have been sentenced to death for all the things you have done wrong. Jesus comes and takes your place.

**The cross shows us that God forgives.** Jesus asks God to forgive the soldiers who nail him to the cross.

**The resurrection shows us that there is life beyond death.** Death is not the end. Jesus has won victory over death and gone to prepare a place for us in heaven. Jesus is alive.

**The resurrection shows us that Jesus is Lord.** He really is God's son. He isn't just another good man who said and did good things. He is God come down to earth to make life with God available to all.

**The resurrection shows that there is purpose to our lives.** Eternal life with God isn't just for when we die. Eternal life is available now for all who put their trust in Jesus. We can know God, through Jesus, today.

## Leaders' notes 5

# The Holy Spirit — our life and breath

### For this session you will need:

* ten objects for the 'Warming up' activity (windmill, hair dryer, teddy, picture of dove, candle, battery, petrol can, glass of water, dictionary, piece of fruit) and two boxes (or carrier bags) to hide them in;
* large sheets of paper and marker pens for brainstorming;
* scrap paper and pens;
* outline of tree (drawn onto a flipchart or poster-sized piece of paper);
* nine fruit shapes each with one of the following words written on them, stuck onto the tree: Love, Joy, Patience, Peace, Generosity, Kindness, Gentleness, Faithfulness, Self-control;
* chopped up pieces of fruit to eat; fruit shapes cut from coloured card (enough for one for each group member).

## home page

The Holy Spirit is God's breath in us, God's life in our life and God's power to help us to live like Jesus. This session looks at who the Holy Spirit is and the effect of the Holy Spirit in our lives.

## warming up

### Conveyor Belt

This game is similar to Kim's Game only a bit whackier! Slide the ten objects, one by one, across a table as if they were moving along a conveyor belt. Hide them in a box or bag at each side of the table so they are only seen for a matter of seconds. (You could play appropriate music as you do this.) Now give out scrap paper and pens and invite group members to list all ten objects from memory.

## logging on

Invite feedback from last week. How much do they remember? How has their opinion of Jesus changed? Did anyone make a cross? Is anyone confused, puzzled or concerned about anything?

Explain that this session is about the Holy Spirit. The last two sessions have focused on God made flesh, God in human form. The Holy Spirit is God the Spirit – God in invisible form.

# The Holy Spirit — our life and breath

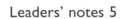

## byte

## Invisible things

Break the group into threes or fours and give each group a big sheet of paper and a marker pen. Introduce the idea that there are many things which are themselves invisible (electricity, for example) but whose *real impact* we can see (e.g. electricity is shown in a working TV!).

Give the young people two minutes to make a list of as many things as possible that are invisible but have visible effects. Invite them to share their lists with the rest of the group.

Some of these things might include: *love, friendship, wind, magnetism, heat, happiness, germs*!

Make the link that although the Holy Spirit is invisible, the impact of the Spirit is evident in our lives and other people's.

## mega byte

## Wind and fire

Read the story of Pentecost, Acts 2:1-13. Set the scene before you read it. The first disciples, before this amazing event, may have been frightened, discouraged, confused or just plain bored. Jesus had told them to wait for the Holy Spirit. They probably had no idea what to expect!

After reading, ask the young people: *If you had been there, what would you have seen? What would you have felt?*

Now talk briefly, *using the ten objects from the warming up game as visual aids*, about some of the things the Holy Spirit is and does:

- On the day of Pentecost the Holy Spirit appeared as wind (*windmill and hairdryer*) and flames of fire (*candle*).

- The Holy Spirit gave the waiting disciples power (*battery and petrol can*).

- Energized and emboldened by the Holy Spirit they were able to speak about Jesus (*dictionary*) in words of many languages.

- Elsewhere in the Bible the Holy Spirit is described as a dove (*dove picture*), refreshing water (*glass of water*), and as a friend who comforts us (*teddy!*)

- That just leaves the fruit …

# The Holy Spirit — our life and breath

## Fruits you!

Hand round the plate of chopped fruit and eat it together as you talk.

Ask the young people what they like about fruit. Is it good? Why is it good?

Show the picture of the tree covered in fruit. Explain that the Bible gives a list of positive qualities that appear in us when the Holy Spirit is at work, just like fruit appearing on a tree.

Read Galatians 5.22-3.

Look at the nine qualities listed and ask the group members:

- Which 'fruit' is most obvious in you now?
- Which fruit could you do with more of?
- Give each person a card fruit shape and a pen. Invite them to write a prayer on it asking God to give them more of the fruit they think they lack.

backing up

The Holy Spirit is not some sort of ghost or spooky thing! Although invisible, the Holy Spirit is as much a part of God as Jesus is. The Holy Spirit gives us life and energy, helps us and strengthens us. The Holy Spirit is God's presence with us.

Jesus promised, 'I will ask the Father to send you the Holy Spirit who will help you and always be with you.' *John 14.16 CEV*

We can get to know the Spirit and welcome the Spirit into our hearts. Then the 'fruits of the Spirit' will begin to be seen in our daily lives.

interfacing

- Use the fruit cards for prayer, inviting each person to read aloud the prayer they have written. (If the group feel uncomfortable reading their own prayers you could collect them into a basket and invite people to pick a card at random so they are reading each other's prayers.)
- Say together the prayer on the handout.

coming soon

Encourage the young people to pray, think and do as outlined on the handout.

**Suggested timings:**

| | |
|---|---|
| Warming up | 10 mins |
| Logging on | 5 mins |
| Byte: Invisible things | 10 mins |
| Megabyte: Wind and fire | 15 mins |
| Byte: Fruits you! | 10 mins |
| Interfacing | 5 mins |
| Backing up/Coming soon | 5 mins |

# The Holy Spirit — our life and breath

## home page

The Holy Spirit is God's breath in us, God's life in our life and God's power to live like Jesus.

## byte

### Invisible things

Although the Holy Spirit is invisible, the impact of the Spirit is evident in the world, in our lives and in the lives of others. We can see the effects of the Holy Spirit – just as we can see the effect of strong wind on trees.

## mega byte

### Wind and fire

When Jesus told his disciples to wait in Jerusalem until God sent the Holy Spirit to give them power they may not have been expecting the events of the day of Pentecost!

On the day of Pentecost all the Lord's followers were together in one place. Suddenly there was a noise from heaven like the sound of a mighty wind! It filled the house where they were meeting. Then they saw what looked like fiery tongues moving in all directions, and a tongue came and settled on each person there. The Holy Spirit took control of everyone, and they began speaking whatever languages the Spirit let them speak …

Everyone was excited and confused. Some of them even kept asking each other, 'What does all this mean?'

Others made fun of the Lord's followers and said, 'They are drunk.'

*Acts 2.1-4, 12-13 CEV*

Imagine you had been there. What would you have seen and felt? Sometimes the Holy Spirit – like the wind – is wild and unpredictable and can make people do surprising things!

>

# The Holy Spirit — our life and breath

## Fruits you!

Inviting the Holy Spirit into our lives may cause all kinds of positive qualities to appear and ripen – like fruit on a tree!

**The fruit of the Spirit is love, joy, peace, patience, kindness, generosity, faithfulness, gentleness, and self-control.**

*Galatians 5.22-3 NRSV*

Look at this list of qualities. Underline the one you think you already have lots of. Now circle the one you think you most need.

In the fruit shape make a note of the prayer you wrote on the back of a piece of fruit.

## interfacing

**Loving God, thank you for the gift of the Holy Spirit.**

**Come into my life and give me your power.**

**Use me to share the love of Jesus with all I meet.**

**Grow in me the fruit of your Holy Spirit. Amen**

## processing

Look for the effect of the Holy Spirit in people's lives – at your church, at school, in your neighbourhood. What do you notice?

## do something about it

Make a kite! Or if you have one, get it out and fly it!

## coming soon

Next week: How to pray.

Part 2

# how christians grow

# prayer — one to one with god

## For this session you will need:

* cards for Guess the Message game;
* photocopy of the Lord's Prayer cut into six pieces;
* paper and pens;
* a picture or model of praying hands (not essential);
* an assortment of beads – different shapes, sizes and colours (NB you could make these on another occasion – see hands-on ideas in Additional resources section, Ways of praying);
* nylon thread or shearing elastic;
* candle and matches;
* Taizé music (or similar);
* Photocopied prayers from the Prayer Helpsheet (pp. 123–4).

### home page

Prayer is about our communication with God and God's communication with us. Focusing specifically on the Lord's Prayer, this session offers practical ways to pray in everyday life.

### warming up

## Guess the Message

Write the messages 'Thank you', 'Please', 'Help!', 'I love you', 'You're cool!', 'Forgive me', 'Meet me', 'I'm sorry', 'Whassup?', 'Call me' on separate pieces of card.

Members of the group choose a card (unseen by other members) and then either:

* act out the message (as in charades or Give us a Clue);
* draw the message (as in Pictionary).

### logging on

Chat about the previous session. Did they notice the Holy Spirit at work anywhere? Did anyone make a kite?

Explain that the Warming up activity was about listening and communication and that this session is about listening to and communicating with God in prayer.

Ask the group members to tell the group (or a partner if the group is large or the members shy):

* when they pray;
* where they pray;
* the weirdest place they've ever prayed!

*(Point out that praying **anywhere** is fine!)*

# prayer — one to one with god

## The Lord's Prayer

When people asked Jesus how they should pray he taught them the Lord's Prayer.

Photocopy the Lord's Prayer and cut it into six chunks. (Our Father . . . your name/Your kingdom . . . in heaven/Give us . . . bread/ Forgive us . . . sin against us/Lead us not . . . evil/For yours . . . Amen.)
Put the pieces of text into a basket and let group members choose one (individually or with a partner). Ask them to think about what their section of the prayer means and to write the meaning in their own words on a separate piece of paper.

Then bring the group back together and read the Lord's Prayer, and the group's interpretation of it, line by line.

Draw attention to the 5Fs summary of the Lord's Prayer on the handout.

## mega byte

## Praying hands

Ask the group to look at their hands (or at a picture of praying hands if available).

Invite them to talk about things they have seen people doing with their hands during prayer. (This may include putting hands together, raising hands, laying hands palm-up on lap or holding something, e.g. a rosary or holding cross.)

Teach the group the following five-finger prayer exercise, which uses the fingers of one hand to give a structure to daily prayer.

**Thumb** (thumbs up) – Thank God for something good.

**Index finger** (pointing) – Ask God to guide you and direct you.

**Middle finger** – Pray for the strong and powerful (e.g. government, world leaders, headteacher).

**Ring finger** – Pray for someone you love.

**Little finger** (pinky!) – Pray for the weak (the ill, lonely, sad or homeless).

# prayer — one to one with god

## byte

### Prayer beads

Explain that holding something in your hand while praying can help focus your thoughts.

Provide the group with an assortment of beads and some thread or elastic. Ask them to choose five beads that they like and then to decide which one might represent the following thing or person to pray for:

- a family member
- a friend
- a place or country in the news;
- a problem or difficulty you face;
- someone who is ill or unhappy.

Invite the group to thread their beads onto a string that they can wear on their wrist or hold when praying.

Encourage the young people to make a note on the handout of who and what they plan to pray for. (Explain that they could also use the five beads to help them pray the 5Fs and five-finger prayers.)

## interfacing

Our thinking so far has all been about the things *we* say to God. But prayer is also about listening.

- Light a candle (or candles) and invite the group to sit in silence.

- Encourage the group to hold and use their prayer beads, praying silently. (You could use some music, e.g. Taizé chants, to help focus attention.)

### Suggested timings:

| | |
|---|---|
| Warming up | 10 mins |
| Logging on | 5 mins |
| Byte: The Lord's Prayer | 15 mins |
| Megabyte: Praying hands | 5 mins |
| Byte: Prayer beads | 15 mins |
| Interfacing | 5 mins |
| Backing up/Coming soon | 5 mins |

## backing up

Prayer is a natural part of life that we can build into our everyday routine. We can speak to God about the things that concern us in ordinary, simple language. We can invite him to be part of our lives, decisions and relationships throughout the day. We can ask him for things, thank him for things or just chat. We can also sit silently in his presence.

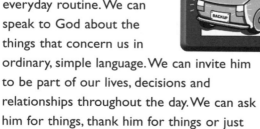

## coming soon

Encourage the group to consider what they are going to pray about during the week, and how and where they are going to do it. Suggest that they use their prayer beads. Give them the opportunity to choose and take away a written prayer from the Additional resources on pages 123–4 to use at home.

# prayer — one to one with god

## home page

Prayer is a one to one with God.

## byte

### The Lord's Prayer

When people asked Jesus how to pray he taught them the Lord's Prayer.

**Father, help us to honour your name.**

**Come and set up your kingdom.**

**Give us each day the food we need.**

**Forgive our sins, as we forgive everyone who has done wrong to us.**

**And keep us from being tempted.**

*Luke 11.2-4 CEV*

The Lord's Prayer can be summarized as 5Fs:

**FATHER** – We address God as Father and acknowledge that he is great and holy.

**FOCUS** – We ask God to focus us on his kingdom, his values, his will.

**FEED** – We ask God to give us our food and all that we need to grow.

**FORGIVE** – We ask God to forgive us and make us forgiving.

**FREE** – We ask God to free us from temptations that entangle us and from evil in the world and in ourselves.

Use the 5Fs to pray this week.

## mega byte

### Praying hands

Sometimes praying is just like chatting to friends – we say whatever is on our mind. But sometimes we might want to make our prayers more structured and organized.

You could use this five-finger prayer to help shape the things you talk to God about.

| | |
|---|---|
| **Something good** | Thumb |
| **Direction** | Index finger |
| **Strong people** | Middle finger |
| **People you love** | Ring finger |
| **Weak people** | Pinky |

## prayer

## Prayer beads

Many people find holding something while praying helps them to focus their thoughts. You could try holding your prayer beads as you pray. Let each bead remind you to pray for a person or place.

| Draw and colour the bead | Who or what will it remind you to pray for? | Write the person, place or thing. |
|---|---|---|
| | A member of your family | |
| | A friend | |
| | A place or country in the news | |
| | A problem or difficulty you face | |
| | Someone you know who is ill or unhappy | |

### interfacing

Use your prayer beads, the 5Fs prayer and the five-finger prayer this week. Which style of praying suits you best?

### processing

This Bible verse tells us to pray all the time!

**Rejoice always, pray without ceasing, give thanks in all circumstances; for this is the will of God in Christ Jesus for you.**

*(1 Thessalonians 5.16-18 NRSV)*

See if you can learn it for next week.

### do something about it

Why not make a special 'Prayer Space' in your bedroom. This could be a cushion or a comfy chair. You could put a cross there (use the one you made after Session 4), a candle (be careful!) an icon, or natural objects such as pebbles or shells, and perhaps a notebook and pen to write down your thoughts.

### coming soon

Next week: The Bible – the world's bestseller!

# The Bible — the world's bestseller

## For this session you will need:

* a collection of different types of book (e.g. cookery books, books of poems, novels, glossy magazines, biographies, encyclopaedias, etc.). Make sure you have several of each type of book;
* the biggest Bible you can find and the smallest one too!
* ten episode cards (photocopied from the supplementary handout and cut up);
* a map, a picture of Christ, a newspaper, a letter, a pen and a lantern (or light bulb);
* ten Bible verses (photocopied from the supplementary handout and cut into strips);
* contemporary translation Bibles to show and lend;
* appropriate Bible notes to show and/or give away (available from Scripture Union, The Good Book Company [formerly St Matthias Press] and the Bible Reading Fellowship).

## home page

The Bible is a great collection of books, written over many hundreds of years by many different authors who lived in many different times and places. It tells the story of God, and especially the story of Jesus. God caused it to be written, and God wants us to read it.

## warming up

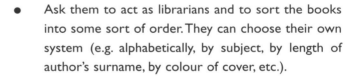

### By the book

* Divide the group into two.
* Give each group a selection of books – cookery books, novels, poetry, etc.
* Ask them to act as librarians and to sort the books into some sort of order. They can choose their own system (e.g. alphabetically, by subject, by length of author's surname, by colour of cover, etc.).
* Invite each group to feed back to the others how they have organized the books and why.

## logging on

Refer back to the last session. Has anyone used their prayer beads? Or tried some new ways of praying?

Explain that the last session focused on what *we* say to God. This session explores how God *speaks to us* through the Bible.

# The Bible — the world's bestseller

## byte

## What's it all about?

Show the group a Bible – as large a one as you can possibly find (and maybe a really small one as well)!

Explain that the Bible is not really one book but a collection of books, like a library. It contains lots of different kinds of books: stories, histories, eyewitness accounts, law books and poetry.

The Bible is in two main parts:

- the Old Testament – telling the story of the people of Israel up until Jesus;
- the New Testament – telling the story of Jesus and the early Church.

Give out the ten episode cards. Which episodes occur in the Old Testament and which in the New? Invite the young people to sort the cards into two categories: Old Testament and New Testament.

Now talk (as concisely and coherently as you can) using the visual aids as illustrations.

- The Old Testament is like a map (*map*) showing us how to live well and find peace with God. It was written over a period of 1,000 years.

- The New Testament is a guide – Jesus (*picture of Christ*).

- It gives us eyewitness accounts of what he did and said (*newspaper*): Matthew, Mark, Luke, John and the Acts of the Apostles – written within 60 years of Jesus' death and resurrection.

- It also contains letters (*letter*), mostly from Paul, written to help new Christians to grow.

- Christians believe that the Bible is inspired by God although it was written down by ordinary human beings (*pen*). Through the Bible God has made his purposes and his personality known.

**Everything in the Scriptures is God's Word. All of it is useful for teaching and helping people and for correcting them and showing them how to live.** (*2 Timothy 3.16 CEV*)

- The Bible is like a lantern (*lantern*). It sheds light and clarity into our lives and guides us on our journey.

**Your word is like a lamp for my feet and a light for my path.** (*Psalm 119.105 NCV*)

## mega byte

## Bestseller

Split the group in two again.

Get the two groups to come up with an advertisement for television to persuade people either to buy a Bible or to read it (or both!). Invite them to consider:

- What are the distinctive qualities about the Bible that could be used to sell it?
- What slogans or striking images can they come up with?

Get the two groups to show their adverts to each other.

# The Bible — the world's bestseller

## byte

### Free sample

- Spread the ten Bible verse cards (photocopied from the supplement) on the floor.

- Invite the young people to walk about reading the verses and to choose the verse they like best or the one that most 'speaks' to them.

- Ask them to copy the verse they have chosen into the box on their handout.

## interfacing

Choose one of *your* favourite bits of the Bible. Read it out and tell the group why it is special or important to you.

Now read it again, ending with the liturgical formula – **This is the word of the Lord.**

Invite the group to respond – **Thanks be to God.**

In some churches it is a tradition to kiss the Bible after it is read in church. This is a sign that when we read the Bible we encounter the living God. If it feels appropriate pass the Bible round for everyone to kiss it. But of course young people may feel embarrassed about doing this. Play it by ear.

## backing up

The Bible is the world's best-selling book. It has been translated into more languages than any other book in history. The Bible's teaching about God and humanity lie at the root of Western culture. It's an amazing book. It is God's word to us. Wouldn't it be a good idea to read it a bit more?

### Suggested timings:

| | |
|---|---|
| Warming up | 10 mins |
| Logging on and feedback | 5 mins |
| Byte: What's it all about? | 15 mins |
| Megabyte: Bestseller | 5 mins |
| Byte: Free sample | 5mins |
| Interfacing | 5 mins |
| Backing up/Coming soon | 5 mins |

## coming soon

- Make sure the group looks at things to pray and do and think about during the week, especially reading the Bible!

- Draw attention to the seven tips in the Be Practical section of the handout.

- Reinforce the point that it is best to read a modern translation of the Bible and show the group a copy of the Youth Bible.

- Have Bibles available to lend; if possible, give away.

- Show copies of some Bible reading notes. Why not give everyone a copy?

# The Bible — the world's bestseller

## home page

The Bible tells the story of God, and especially the story of Jesus. God caused it to be written, and God wants us to read it.

## byte

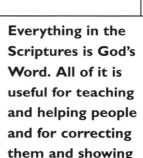

## What's it all about?

The Bible is like a library. There are lots of different types of book in it – stories, histories, eyewitness accounts, law books, poetry and letters.

There are two main parts:

- The Old Testament – telling the story of the people of Israel up until Jesus.
- The New Testament – telling the story of Jesus and the early Church.

### Direct Line

Christians believe that the Bible, although it was written down by ordinary human beings, is inspired by God. Through the Bible, God has made his purposes and his personality known.

- The Old Testament is like a map, showing us how to live well and find peace with God. It was written over a period of 1,000 years.

- The New Testament is a guide. It shows us Jesus. It gives us eyewitness accounts of what he did and said: Matthew, Mark, Luke, John and the Acts of the Apostles – written within 60 years of Jesus' death and resurrection.

- It also contains letters, mostly from Paul, written to help new Christians to grow.

> **Everything in the Scriptures is God's Word. All of it is useful for teaching and helping people and for correcting them and showing them how to live.**
>
> *2 Timothy 3.16 CEV*

## byte

## Free sample

The Bible describes itself as a light which helps us to see how to live.

> **Your word is like a lamp for my feet and a light for my path.**
>
> *Psalm 119.105 NCV*

continued >

# the Bible — the world's bestseller

## byte

*continued >*

Write the Bible verse you chose here in the box ...

*Read it during the week and see what a difference it makes!*

## Be practical

Here are 7 tips to help you read your Bible:

1. Read a modern version you can understand.

2. Don't try to read it from cover to cover, or use it as a lucky dip.

3. Pray that God will help you to understand what you read.

4. Try to listen to what God is saying to you as you read it.

5. Use your imagination. What must it have been like for the people involved?

6. Try using Bible notes. They help you read and understand the Bible.

7. Read a little bit and then think. Don't expect to understand everything all of the time to understand everything all of the time.

## interfacing

Read the verse you wrote in the Free Sample box each day before you pray.

## processing

What is *your* favourite bit of the Bible and why?

Come along next week ready to tell people.

## do something about it

Read a Bible! Try a chunk of Mark or Luke or try out some Bible notes.

## coming soon

Next week: God's people, the Church.

# The Bible — the world's bestseller

## Episode cards

| | |
|---|---|
| **The creation of the world** | **Moses and the Ten Commandments** |
| **Paul's letter to the Romans** | **Jonah and the whale** |
| **Feeding the 5,000** | **Noah's ark** |
| **Jesus dies on the cross** | **The coming of the Holy Spirit** |
| **The birth of Jesus** | **Joseph and his amazing technicolour coat** |

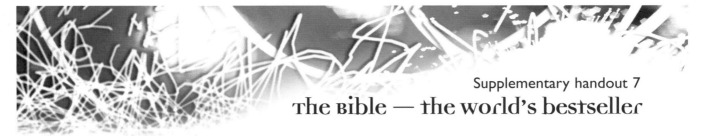

# the bible — the world's bestseller

## Free sample – Bible verses

> God is our mighty fortress, always ready to help in times of trouble.
>
> *Psalm 46.1 CEV*

> Don't be afraid. I am with you. Don't tremble with fear. I am your God.
>
> *Isaiah 41.10 CEV*

> As a deer gets thirsty for streams of water, I truly am thirsty for you, my God.
>
> *Psalm 42.1 CEV*

> Jesus said, 'I will be with you always, even until the end of the world.'
>
> *Matthew 28.20 CEV*

> God loved the people of this world so much that he gave his only Son, so that everyone who has faith in him will have eternal life and never really die.
>
> *John 3.16 CEV*

> Jesus said, 'A thief comes only to rob, kill, and destroy. I came so that everyone would have life, and have it fully.'
>
> *John 10.10 CEV*

> God showed how much he loved us by having Christ die for us, even though we were sinful.
>
> *Romans 5.8 CEV*

> Paul writes, 'I ask the glorious Father and God of our Lord Jesus Christ to give you his Spirit. The Spirit will make you wise and let you understand what it means to know God.'
>
> *Ephesians 1.17 CEV*

> God is love.
>
> *1 John 4.16 CEV*

> God says, 'Listen! I am standing and knocking at your door. If you hear my voice and open the door, I will come in and we will eat together.'
>
> *Revelation 3.20 CEV*

# The church — what a great body!

## home page

As followers of Jesus we aren't meant to 'go it alone'. We need each other.

The Church is simply Christians meeting together with other Christians. It is people – the people of God – not bricks and stones. This session explores what it means to be a part of the Body of Christ – where everybody matters and we each have a part to play.

**For this session you will need:**

* ten word 'bricks' photocopied from the supplementary handout and cut out (enough for one between two);
* large pieces of paper and marker pens;
* smaller sheets of paper and felt pens or crayons;
* blindfolds, bibs (or old shirts), spoons and bowls of cereal or jelly (enough for one between three);
* sweets resembling body parts;
* Jenga or similiar, if you're not use the messy Warming up.

## warming up

Choose one of the following (depending on how much mess you can stand!).

### 1. Feeding Frenzy

* Get into groups of 3.

* Person 1 wears a blindfold and a bib and has hands behind back.

* Person 2 sits behind Person 1 with arms through Person 1's armpits.

* Person 3 gives instructions to 1 and 2.

* Person 2 must feed Person 1 with cereal or jelly with instructions from Person 3!

Make the point that normally we perform all three functions without thinking about it. Bodies work well when the parts are working together as one!

### 2. Jenga

Play a game like Jenga or Uno Stacko which requires bricks to be built together into a tower.

Like the bricks, we need each other's support.

## logging on

Chat about the last session. How have the young people got on with their Bible reading? Has anyone got anything to report?

Explain that this session is about the Church – what is it for, what is it like and how do we fit in?

# the church — what a great body!

## What's the point?

What is the Church and what is it for? This activity looks at things we do in church and asks the young people to rank them in order of importance. (There are no right answers!)

- In pairs, give group members ten words or phrases (photocopied from the supplementary handout and cut into 'bricks').

- Ask them to lay the 'bricks' on the floor in a tower with the thing they consider *most* important at the top of the tower and the thing they consider *least* important at the bottom. (They can have more than one 'brick' on each level if they consider some things of equal importance.)

- Invite the group to feed back their results.

What is their own experience of being part of the Church? What is good? What is not so good?

## Design–a–Church

- Split the group into threes or fours.

- Give each group a large sheet of paper and a marker pen.

- Tell them to design a brand new church building that reflects their priorities — what they consider to be important about the Church.

- Encourage them to think about how space should be used, what facilities to include and even decor and atmosphere.

- Get each group to show the others its design.

We sometimes think of Church as a building — something we *go* to.

In fact we *are* the Church — the people. The building is just a convenient place to meet.

The first church building did not appear until about 200 years after Jesus. Before that Christians met together in each other's homes.

This is what Luke said the early Church was like:

**All the Lord's followers often met together, and they shared everything they had. They would sell their property and possessions and give the money to whoever needed it . . . They broke bread together in different homes and shared their food happily and freely, while praising God.**

*Acts 2.44-7 CEV*

How similar is your church?

# The church — what a great body!

## mega byte

## Body parts

(You could eat sweets resembling body parts as you do this activity!)

Whenever we say 'the Peace' in church we say this: 'We are the body of Christ.'

Bodies are made up of different parts working together as one unit.

Belonging to the Church is like being part of a body — a living, organic, growing body.

Just as all the parts of a body are needed for a body to function healthily, so each person makes a contribution to the whole Church.

- Give each group member a piece of paper and a marker pen.

- Ask them to think about what they are good at, what special talent they have, or what gifts they think they have.

- Encourage them to see this talent or gift in terms of a body part. For example: Hand – someone who is good at making things; Brain – someone who is good at having ideas; Eye – someone who is good at spotting when someone is in difficulty and needs help; Knee – someone who is good at praying; Mouth – someone who is good at speaking or singing; Heart – someone who is very loving; Pancreas – someone unseen but very important. (You may need to censor some of their suggestions!)

- Ask them to draw the body part that represents themselves.

## interfacing

Use the body part drawings.

- Sit in a circle.

- The leader says: 'The Church is the body of Christ.'

- Then each group member holds up their drawing and says: 'This is a (whichever part it is). I offer my (whatever the gift or talent is).'

- End by sharing the Peace:

*continued >*

# the church — what a great body!

## interfacing

*continued >*

**We are the body of Christ.**

**In the one Spirit we were all baptized into one body.**

**Let us then pursue all that makes for peace and builds up our common life.**

**The peace of the Lord be always with you.**

*And also with you.*

> *Common Worship: Services and Prayers for the Church of England*
> (Church House Publishing, 2000), *p. 290.*

## backing up

The Church is not a building but a body. We are all part of the Church – part of the Body of Christ. We all have things to offer and gifts to share. The Church is like a family. Like all families it is far from perfect and needs working at. But everyone is important. We need each other in order to grow as Christians.

## coming soon

Encourage the group to look at the things suggested on the handout to process, interface and do.

### Suggested timings:

| | |
|---|---|
| Warming up | 10 mins |
| Logging on and feedback | 5 mins |
| Byte: What's the point? | 10 mins |
| Byte: Design-a-Church | 15 mins |
| Megabyte: Body parts | 10 mins |
| Interfacing | 5 mins |
| Backing up/Coming soon | 5 mins |

# the church — what a great body!

The Church is not a building but a body. We are all part of the Church – part of the Body of Christ.

**byte**

## What's the point?

What is the Church for? What do you like most about your church?

Is there anything you dislike?

In the box, write down what *you* think are the *three most important things* a Church should be.

In my opinion Church should be:

1.

2.

3.

**byte**

## Design–a–Church

Church isn't a place you go to, it's people.

The first church building didn't appear until about 200 years after Jesus. Before that Christians just met in each other's homes for prayer and worship.

This is what Luke said the early Church was like:

**All the Lord's followers often met together, and they shared everything they had. They would sell their property and possessions and give the money to whoever needed it ... They broke bread together in different homes and shared their food happily and freely, while praising God.**

*Acts 2.44-7 CEV*

What would you change to make your church more like the early Church?

# The church — what a great body!

**mega byte**

## Body parts

The Church is the Body of Christ.

Bodies are made up of different parts working together as one unit.
Belonging to the Church is like being part of a body – a living, organic, growing body.
Just as all the parts of a body are needed for a body to function healthily, so each
person makes a contribution to the whole Church.

What do you feel is your own special talent or gift?

Make a note of the body part you drew and why.

**interfacing**

Like all families we don't always find getting along together easy.

Pray for other people in your church – especially those you don't
like very much. Ask God to help you appreciate them.

**processing**

What would a
visiting stranger think
of your church?

**do something about it**

Use your talent this
week to help others.

**coming soon**

Next week:
Holy Communion
– bread of life.

# the church — what a great body!

| | |
|---|---|
| **Praying** | **Worshipping and singing** |
| **Eating** | **Reading the Bible** |
| **Relaxing** | **Learning** |
| **Encountering God** | **Making friends** |
| **Helping each other** | **Receiving communion** |

# нoly communion — the bread of life

The service that we call Holy Communion is the one service that Jesus gave us. It is sometimes called the Eucharist. It is a celebration and a living encounter with the risen Lord. We are not just remembering what Jesus did in the past, we are meeting him in the present and preparing for our future with him.

## For this session you will need:

* to make some bread! Don't panic, it is not as difficult as you might think, and a recipe and ingredients are printed at the end of these leaders' notes;

* large pieces of paper, coloured pens, paper, scissors, glue, etc. for making posters;

* copies of the printed prayer (one each) photocopied from the supplementary handout.

## Breadmaking

It is possible (just!) to make, bake and eat some bread in an hour, but you need to be well organized. Unless you make this session slightly longer (which is always an option) it is best to *make the dough before the young people arrive* (see notes).

Having made the dough get the young people round a table (hands washed, sleeves rolled up) and give each person a chunk of dough. You will need to knead the dough for about ten minutes.

As you knead the bread dough do the Logging on section and the chat about parties at the start of Byte: Party Time.

Invite the young people to share what they have been praying about, thinking about and doing as a result of the last session. Be ready to contribute your own (brief!) reflections.

Introduce this session and explain that it is about Holy Communion – when we meet Jesus in bread and wine.

# Holy communion — the bread of life

byte

## Party time

Introduce the subject of parties and celebrations by asking the questions:

- What's the best party you have ever been to?

- What makes a good party?

- What are the special occasions and times of the year when we have parties?

You should by now have been kneading the dough for about 10 minutes. Ask each young person to shape their dough into two small bread rolls. Now the dough should be ready to be left to rise (see instructions) for about 25–30 minutes.

*Pre-heat your oven!*

At this point in the session it would be good (if possible) to move to another space.

Continue with this brief input (no more than 5 minutes) about the Eucharist.

Put it into your own words, using language that will be familiar to the young people from the church and tradition you are part of.

These are the main points to make:

- **Last Supper** – On the night before he died Jesus broke bread and drank wine with his friends.

- **Breaking bread** – Jesus did this to help his friends understand his death. Like the bread, his body was going to be broken and, like the wine, his blood was going to be poured out.

- **Remembering** – Jesus told his friends to break bread and drink wine together as a way of remembering him. After Jesus rose from the dead his disciples would have remembered his strange words at the Last Supper – 'This is my body, this is my blood, do this to remember me' – and come to realize that this was a way they could know his presence with them.

- **Thank you** – The word 'Eucharist' means Thanksgiving in Greek (the language the New Testament was written in). Holy Communion, Mass and the Last Supper are other words used for this service which celebrates and gives thanks for what Jesus has done in dying on the cross and rising again.

byte

## Everyone's invited!

The Eucharist isn't just about remembering past events. It is a living encounter with Jesus.

In the Eucharist we encounter Jesus in three ways:

- **In the Bible** – the first part of the communion service (often called the Liturgy of the Word).

*continued >*

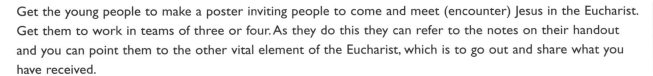

## byte

*continued >*

- **In sharing bread and wine** – the second part of the service (often called the Liturgy of the Sacrament).

- **In each other** – the sharing of the Peace that comes in the middle of the service.

Get the young people to make a poster inviting people to come and meet (encounter) Jesus in the Eucharist. Get them to work in teams of three or four. As they do this they can refer to the notes on their handout and you can point them to the other vital element of the Eucharist, which is to go out and share what you have received.

Twenty minutes into this activity, take a break to put the bread rolls in the oven. They only need 15 minutes.

Get each group to display and talk about their poster.

- What aspects of the Eucharist have they emphasized?

- What is it about encountering Jesus in the Eucharist that they want to share?

- What questions do they have?

## backing up

The Eucharist or Holy Communion is the main act of worship for the Christian Church, a service given by Jesus himself so that we can understand what his death and resurrection mean and carry on meeting him and being fed by him.

The supplementary handout for this session outlines the structure of the Eucharist. This will be useful to use with groups where the young people are preparing for confirmation, or to receive Holy Communion for the first time. Used in conjunction with the service book for your church it explains how the service fits together and what the different parts mean.

## coming soon

Encourage the young people to think about what they are going to pray about, think about and act upon as a result of this week's session.

By now the bread should be ready to come out of the oven.

**Suggested timings:**

| | |
|---|---|
| Logging on and feedback | 5 mins |
| Byte: Party time | 15 mins |
| Byte: Everyone's invited! | 30 mins |
| Backing up/Coming soon | 5 mins |
| Interfacing | 5 mins |

# Holy communion — the bread of life

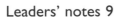

*(This week, leave the Prayer activity till the very end so that the bread is cooked and ready.)*

● Put the bread rolls in a basket on the floor.

● Put the posters around the bread and light a candle. Sit on the floor around the bread.

● Use the set prayers printed on the supplementary handout or make up your own prayer thanking God for feeding us with Jesus, the bread of life.

● Eat a roll of bread as you pray.

● Invite the young people to take their second bread roll home to share with someone else (see handout).

---

## A simple recipe for bread rolls  *Ingredients (for about 12 rolls):*

| | | | | | |
|---|---|---|---|---|---|
| 650 g (1 lb 5 oz) | White bread flour | 5 ml (1 tsp) | Sugar | 17 g sachet | Yeast |
| 10 ml (2 tsp) | Salt | 15 g (1/2 oz) | Hard white vegetable fat or lard | 400 ml (14 fl oz) | Warm water (1 part boiling, 2 parts cold) |

## Directions:

1. Grease and warm a baking sheet.

2. In a warm bowl mix flour, salt and sugar. Rub in fat and stir in yeast.

3. Add warm water and mix to a soft dough.

*If you are making the rolls as part of a standard length one-hour session you will need to have reached this stage before the young people arrive.*

4. Knead the dough by stretching and folding for about ten minutes on a warm, floured surface.

5. Shape into balls and place on the baking sheet.

*While you are doing this you can talk about what they have done since last week and about parties.*

6. Cover dough loosely with clingfilm and leave for about 25-30 minutes in a warm, draught-free place, like an airing cupboard, or on top of the cooker. Let the dough rise. (It should roughly double in size.)

7. Pre-heat the oven to 240° C (475° F, Gas mark 9).

*Now do the Party Time input and the Everyone's Invited poster activity, breaking off after 30 minutes to:*

8. Place the rolls in the middle of the pre-heated oven and immediately turn the temperature down to 230° C (450° F, Gas mark 8). Bake for 15 minutes.

*Now you finish the poster activity and complete the session up till the final prayers.*

9. Remove from the oven and turn onto a wire tray. If bottom crust sounds hollow when tapped, the bread is cooked. Leave to cool.

*Just enough time for the final prayer together, with rolls to be eaten nice and hot and taken home and shared.*

# Holy communion — the bread of life

## home page

Holy Communion is the main act of worship for the Christian Church. It is a service given by Jesus himself so that we can understand what his death and resurrection mean and carry on meeting him and being fed by him. Sometimes it is called the Eucharist.

## byte

### Party time

Jesus gave us Holy Communion. That's why it is the main act of worship for the Christian Church.

- **Last Supper** – On the night before he died Jesus broke bread and drank wine with his friends.

- **Breaking bread** – Jesus did this to help his friends understand his death. Like the bread, his body was going to be broken and, like the wine, his blood was going to be poured out.

- **Remembering** – Jesus told his friends to break bread and drink wine together as a way of remembering him. After Jesus rose from the dead his disciples would have remembered his strange words at the Last Supper – 'This is my body, this is my blood, do this to remember me' – and come to realize that this was a way they could know his presence with them.

- **Thank you** – The word 'Eucharist' means Thanksgiving in Greek (the language the New Testament was written in). Holy Communion, Mass and the Last Supper are other words used for this service which celebrates and gives thanks for what Jesus has done in dying on the cross and rising again.

## byte

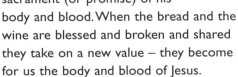

### Everyone's invited!

In the Eucharist we encounter Jesus in three ways:

- **In the Bible.** We cannot hear Jesus speaking to us today as people could when he was alive on earth, but we can hear him speak through the Bible. Through readings from the Bible and the sermon God teaches and encourages us in our faith.

- **In bread and wine.** We cannot experience Jesus feeding us like he fed the five thousand or had supper with his friends, but he does feed us when we share bread and wine. Jesus promised he would always be with his people. One of the ways he is with us is through the sacrament (or promise) of his body and blood. When the bread and the wine are blessed and broken and shared they take on a new value – they become for us the body and blood of Jesus.

*continued >*

# ʜoly communion — the bread of life

## byte

*continued >*

- **In each other.**
  We cannot feel Jesus holding us or blessing us physically, but we can feel his love through other people. The sharing of the Peace is the sign of our belonging to each other as God's people.

## byte

## Share it!

But this isn't the end of the Eucharist. The final prayer says this:

**Almighty God,**

**we thank you for feeding us**

**with the body and blood of your Son Jesus Christ.**

**Through him we offer you our souls and bodies**

**to be a living sacrifice.**

**Send us out**

**in the power of your Spirit**

**to live and work**

**to your praise and glory. Amen.**

*Common Worship: Services and Prayers for the Church of England* (Church House Publishing, 2000), *p. 182.*

We are sent out to share with others the good things we have received. The Eucharist is a party to celebrate our faith. But we have also been issued with invitations to give to everyone.

What is it about meeting Jesus in the Eucharist that you want to share with others? How might you do this?

## interfacing

Pray for the many people in the world who do not have enough food to eat.

## processing

Where else might we encounter Jesus this week? Think about the different ways we can hear, experience and be challenged by Jesus in our daily lives.

## do something about it

Take your second bread roll home and share it with someone else.

## coming soon

Next week: Becoming a Christian.

# The structure of Holy Communion or the Eucharist

## The Gathering

- The priest and people greet each other in the Lord's name.

- Everyone confesses his or her sins and is assured of God's forgiveness.

- Silence is kept and there is a Collect (a set prayer for that day).

## The Liturgy of the Word

- The priest and people proclaim and respond to the word of God. There is always a reading from the Gospels, and usually one or two others from the Old and New Testament.

- There is usually a sermon explaining and exploring the meaning of God's word for our lives today.

- On Sundays the Creed is said. The Creed is a summary of what Christians believe.

- There are prayers of intercession for the Church, the creation, human society, the local community and those who suffer. We remember those who have died. We join our prayers with the saints'.* (* In some parts of the Christian tradition, all Christians who have died are referred to as 'saints' and it's believed that they pray with us and for us in heaven.)

## The Liturgy of the Sacrament

- The priest and people exchange a sign of Peace.

- The table is prepared. Bread and wine are placed upon it. There is usually a collection.

- The Eucharistic Prayer is the climax of the Eucharist. The priest takes the bread and wine and gives thanks to God for all that he has done in the creation and salvation of the world. This great prayer gathers together all the prayers and thanksgivings that we offer to God. At the centre of the prayer we remember what Jesus said and did at the Last Supper.

- The Lord's Prayer.

- The breaking of the bread.

- Receiving Communion. In the Church of England you either have to be confirmed, or have been given permission to receive communion. If you don't receive communion you can come forward to receive a blessing.

# The structure of Holy communion or the Eucharist

## The Dismissal

- The priest and people say a prayer after communion.

- The priest announces God's blessing on his people.

- We are all sent out to love and serve the Lord.

Get hold of a copy of the service book from your church, see the different prayers, and familiarize yourself with this service.

## A prayer you could use in this session

Different people can say the lines of this prayer in plain type and everyone joins in the words printed in bold.

Jesus said, I am the bread of life, anyone who comes
to me shall not hunger,

Anyone who believes in me shall never thirst.

**Alleluia! Lord, give us this bread always.**

The bread of God comes down from heaven,

And gives life to the world.

**Alleluia! Lord, give us this bread always.**

Anyone who eats my flesh and drinks my blood has eternal life

And I will raise them up on the last day.

**Alleluia! Lord, give us this bread always.**

Adapted from *Enriching the Christian Year* compiled
by Michael Perham (SPCK, 1993), p. 208.

# Becoming a christian — stand up and be counted

This session draws together the threads of the previous nine sessions and asks the questions What is a Christian? Are you a Christian? What will be the implications for you of following Jesus? The session gives group members the opportunity to mark their own spiritual journey and, if they are ready, to make a conscious commitment to Christ.

## For this session you will need:

* sheets of newspaper and music or a coin (depending on the Warming up activity you choose);
* card cut into fish shapes (enough for one each) plus net (optional);
* pens;
* three Stand and Deliver cards (photocopied from the supplementary handout);
* a collection of decent-sized rocks (enough for one each) to build a cairn;
* song words or tape/CD of 'Will You Come and Follow Me?' (see p. 61).

## warming up

Play one of these games about standing.

### 1. Newspaper Islands

Spread sheets of newspaper (enough for one each) on the floor and play music. When the music stops the young people have to stand on a sheet of paper. Each time you start the music again reduce the number of sheets and the size of each sheet so that the newspaper islands get smaller and more sparse. Eliminate those who fail to find an island to stand on or who fall off their island. See how tiny a sheet can still be stood upon!

### 2. Heads and Tails

Tell group members to stand up and to select heads (hands on head) or tails (hands on bottoms). Toss a coin. If it is heads all those who have chosen heads remain standing. The others are out and have to sit down. Keep playing until only one player is left. That person is the winner. (Give them the coin as a prize!)

## logging on

Explain that the Warming up involved standing, and that this session is about standing up, standing firm and making a stand. This might be a good point at which to chat to the group about how they have felt about the course so far. Explain that the nine previous sessions have explored what Christians believe and that this tenth session gives them the opportunity to make a decision about what *they* believe. Great sensitivity should be shown by leaders at this point so that the invitation to 'stand up' isn't given in a pressurized or manipulative way. (For groups using *Youth Emmaus* as a preparation for confirmation, the supplementary handout ties this session more closely to the confirmation liturgy.)

# Becoming a christian — stand up and be counted

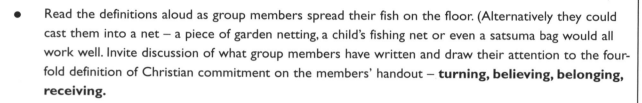

## Fishy business

byte

- Give each member of the group a card fish. Explain that a fish was used as a secret symbol amongst early Christians whose lives were often endangered by their faith.

- Ask the group to write on one side of the fish their own definition of what a Christian is.

- Read the definitions aloud as group members spread their fish on the floor. (Alternatively they could cast them into a net – a piece of garden netting, a child's fishing net or even a satsuma bag would all work well. Invite discussion of what group members have written and draw their attention to the four-fold definition of Christian commitment on the members' handout – **turning, believing, belonging, receiving.**

(NB The supplementary handout links this definition with the confirmation promises and responses in *Common Worship*.)

## Follow me

mega byte

- Read together the story of the rich young man (Mark 10: 17-22).

- Ask the group to fill in the speech bubbles on the members' handout. Then get them to read aloud what they have written.

Explain that Jesus said 'Follow me!' to the young man and he says it to us. We have a choice whether we follow or not. Some of us make that choice gradually over a long period of time. Some of us make it at a particular moment that we can mark and look back on. If members of the group are being confirmed explain that they are making that choice at their confirmation. If you are not using the course as confirmation preparation suggest that members of the group might like to make the choice to follow Jesus during this session.

## Stand and deliver

byte

Before group members decide whether they want to be Christians it is important that they know that following Jesus will have an impact on many aspects of their lives. This activity aims to show group members that following Jesus (far from being an easy escapist option as some critics suggest) can sometimes be tough.

- Divide the young people into three groups.

- Give each group one of the Stand and Deliver cards photocopied from the supplementary handout.

*continued >*

# becoming a christian — stand up and be counted

## byte

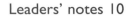

*continued >*

- Give them five minutes to read, discuss and respond to the life described on the card and then ask them to tell the other two groups about the person described. (If the group are quite extrovert they might like to 'act out' the information on the card rather than just talk about it.)

Now draw the group's attention to the list of lifestyle implications on their handout. Ask them to tick all the things that they think will be affected by their decision to follow Jesus.

Explain that some of these issues will be looked at more fully in the next few sessions of the course.

## interfacing

- As an introduction to prayer sing together 'Will You Come and Follow Me?' (Iona Community, 1986) or listen to it sung. (The song can be found on 'A Touching Place', Wild Goose Worship Group, 1986.)

- Invite the group to read through the commitment prayer on their handout and decide whether they feel ready to pray it.

- Say the prayer together.

- Explain that paths and routes (especially in mountains) are often marked by cairns – piles of stones beside the path – and that walkers sometimes add their own stones to the cairn as they pass by. Invite the group to take a rock and place it on a cairn as a sign that they are marking their spiritual journey. (You could play some music while group members do this. This will probably work best if you have already built a small cairn that the young people can add to.)

## backing up

- Jesus calls us to follow him.

- We choose whether or not to respond.

- If we decide 'Yes' this choice affects the way we live our lives and will influence the people we become.

- Following Jesus involves standing up and being counted.

- Jesus stands by us as we stand up for him.

## coming soon

Encourage group members to read the list of lifestyle implications on their handout and think more deeply about these in the coming week. Suggest that they pray the commitment prayer daily.

### Suggested timings:

| | |
|---|---|
| Warming up | 5 mins |
| Logging on | 5 mins |
| Byte: Fishy business | 10 mins |
| Megabyte: Follow me! | 10 mins |
| Byte: Stand and deliver | 15 mins |
| Interfacing | 10 mins |
| Backing up/Coming soon | 5 mins |

# Becoming a christian — stand up and be counted

Jesus calls us to follow him. We choose whether to respond or not. If we decide 'yes' this choice affects the way we live our lives and will influence the people we become.

## Being a Christian involves:

**TURNING** – away from a self-centred lifestyle and from everything evil.

**BELIEVING** – that God loves you and Jesus died for you.

**BELONGING** – to God's family, the Church.

**RECEIVING** – the gifts and power of the Holy Spirit to help you live like Jesus.

## Follow me!

A rich young man came to Jesus and asked him what he needed to do to enter God's kingdom. Jesus told him to sell all his possessions, give the money away and then follow him. Read the story in Mark 10.17-22.

This was too much for the young man! The Bible says he walked away sad. But notice, Jesus carries on loving him.

Write in the bubbles (in your own words):

● what the young man said to himself as he walked away;

● what Jesus was thinking.

Jesus calls us to follow him. Like the rich young man we have a choice to say 'Yes' or 'No'. Some Christians make that choice gradually over months or years. Others make it at a specific moment in time and can remember a date and a place (like a first kiss!). What choice will *you* make?

›

# Becoming a christian — stand up and be counted

## byte

## Stand and deliver!

Critics of Christianity sometimes say it is a soft option, an escape from reality. The lives of Christian people show that this is far from true! There is a real *cost* involved in being a Christian. Saying 'Yes' to following Jesus can mean our lives are never the same again!

Tick the things in the list below that you think will be affected by your decision to follow Jesus:

- ○ The way I treat my friends and family
- ○ The language I use
- ○ My response to global poverty
- ○ My attitude to sex
- ○ The way I spend my spare time

- ○ My attitude to race
- ○ The things I watch on TV
- ○ The way I wear my hair
- ○ The way I treat people I don't like
- ○ The things I spend my money on.

We'll be looking more fully at some of these issues in the next few sessions of the course.

## A commitment prayer

Read through this prayer. It is strong stuff, isn't it? Only pray it if you mean it!

**Dear Jesus,**

**Thank you that you are calling me to follow you.**

**Thank you that you loved me enough to die for me.**

**Thank you that you show me how to live.**

**Forgive all I've done and said and thought that has been wrong.**

**Help me to turn from selfish ways and all that is evil and to live in your light.**

**Fill me with the Holy Spirit so that I can have the strength to live as a Christian.**

**Take my life and use me to let your kingdom come on earth.**

**Amen.**

# Becoming a Christian — stand up and be counted

## interfacing

If you prayed the commitment prayer during this session pray it again at home every day this week. (If you didn't feel ready to pray it, talk to God about why and ask him to help you find out more.)

## processing

Read the list of things above and think more deeply about how some of them may affect you.

## do something about it

Ask some of the older people in your church what difference being a Christian makes in their lives. You might be surprised by the answers they give!

## coming soon

Next week: Your kingdom come . . .

# stand and deliver cards

### Oscar Romero

As Archbishop of El Salvador, Oscar Romero worked for peace and the recognition of human rights. He told the truth about the injustice present in his country and its government. Speaking out for what he believed to be right won him the Nobel Peace Prize and many enemies. In 1980 he was assassinated, shot dead during a Communion service.

### Mother Teresa

Mother Teresa became a nun at the age of 18. When she was 38, in 1948, she believed that God was calling her to work amongst the sick and dying poor of the city of Calcutta. She gave the rest of her life to caring for the poorest of the poor and died in 1997. She once said: 'I see God in every human being. When I wash the leper's wounds I feel I am nursing the Lord himself.'

### Tom

Tom is 14 and lives in Bournemouth. He did the *Youth Emmaus* course at his local church and decided he wanted to follow Jesus. Tom is the only Christian in his school football team. Some of his mates tease him for going to church. They laugh at him and say God is just for wimps. But they've also noticed that Tom always plays fair and never badmouths the ref.

# Anglican confirmation

home page

### Supplement for groups where young people are being prepared for Anglican confirmation

This supplement ties the contents of Session Ten more closely to the Anglican confirmation liturgy and is designed for use by those groups that are using *Youth Emmaus* as a preparation for confirmation.

(All page numbers have been taken from *Common Worship: Initiation Services*, Church House Publishing, 1998.)

byte

## Fishy business

In this activity group members are invited to think about what a Christian is.

The handout lists *four* elements of becoming, or being a Christian: **Turning, Believing, Belonging, Receiving**. Draw attention to the ways in which these four things are mentioned in the confirmation service.

### 1. Turning

In confirmation the bishop will invite the young people to reject the devil, renounce evil and turn to Christ (p. 125).

### 2. Believing

A statement of faith or creed about God, Jesus and the Holy Spirit will be made by the whole congregation during the service (p. 127).

Confirmation candidates are asked:

**Are you ready with your own mouth and from your own heart to affirm your faith in Jesus Christ?** (p. 124)

### 3. Belonging

After the confirmation the young people are welcomed by the congregation with the words: **We welcome you into the fellowship of faith, we are children of the same heavenly Father; we welcome you.** (p. 131)

### 4. Receiving

During the service the bishop prays for the young people to receive the power of the Holy Spirit. He says (addressing God): **Let your Holy Spirit rest upon them ...** (p. 129)

The whole congregation recognize their own need for God's empowering help to live as Christians when they say: **With the help of God, we will** (p. 125)

›

## Stand and deliver

In this activity the group are encouraged to see the lifestyle implications of their decision to follow Christ.

The confirmation liturgy in *Common Worship* commissions confirmation candidates to live out their faith in specific ways (pp.130-31). These include:

- commitment to attend worship and Holy Communion/ the Eucharist;

- resisting evil;

- proclamation of the good news in word and example;

- serving others;

- involvement in the world.

(Some of these challenges will be examined more closely in the last five sessions of the course.)

You might want to read this section of liturgy together as a group in place of the commitment prayer. Giving the young people copies of this part of the confirmation service to take home and think about would be appropriate at this stage.

# optional session — нot potatoes!

## home page

This is a one-off session which aims to tackle some of the thorny questions that often arise during a course like *Youth Emmaus*.

You could use this session at any point during the course: as a break, part-way through, or at the end, as a celebration of getting through the course – or not at all.

The format is looser than in previous sessions and can be adapted to suit the needs and maturity level of your group. It needs to feel different from the other sessions.

Start with food – baked potatoes would be an obvious choice!

We have given you ideas of how to deal with three issues, but of course you may use this session to deal with other questions that have come up.

Three Hot Potatoes which are likely to come up are:

- If God is so good, why is there so much suffering?

- Whose God is it anyway? What about other faiths?

- Heaven and hell – what happens when I die?

There is no handout for this session.

### For this session you will need:

* paper and pens;
* food and drink – baked potatoes or some sort of meal to share. You could get the young people to bring their own food, or even to organize the whole of the catering side of the evening.

## warming up

### Chat show

You are a chat show host, and God is your special guest. You only have time to ask *one* question. What would your one question be?

Get everyone to write down their question. You may also add in questions that have come up in previous sessions but have not yet been dealt with properly.

byte

# The big issues

There are a number of ways to get the discussions going. Either deal with the questions as they arise, sharing ideas in the group or invite a panel of people from your church to help address the questions.

If you decide to concentrate on the three hot potatoes we have identified try the following:

- **Points of View:** Photocopy the Help Sheets (pages 73–6) onto card and cut them up. Distribute them among group members and ask the young people to read out the point of view on each card. Make sure you keep cards for each issue separate!

- **Spin the Knife:** put the Points of View cards in a large circle on the floor with a knife in the centre. Spin the knife and get the group to discuss whichever sttement to which the knife points. Repeat this as many times as you like.

- **Bullet Points:** Photocopy pages 70–72 and make three sheets of bullet points – one for each issue. Give copies of the sheets to the young people, one issue at a time. Ask them to read the bullet points. Which arguments do they agree or disagree with? Invite them to read aloud the viewpoint that convinces them most.

- **On the Spot:** choose an issue for debate and a chairperson/referee to keep the peace. Invite one person to argue his or her corner on your chosen subject for two minutes, and then someone else to put an opposing point of view on the same subject. Now invite members of the 'audience' to add their own comments. Finally take an audience vote for or against the initial viewpoint.

Whichever format you choose, try to allow plenty of space for discussion.

byte

## 1. If God is so good why is there so much suffering?

*Ever looked at the TV when there has been a tragedy and thought: Why?*
*Ever wondered if God intends us to suffer?*
*Ever wondered where God was in all the suffering we see in the world?*

- We have been given the freedom to choose between right and wrong. The story of Adam and Eve illustrates this.

- Much suffering is caused by human beings' greed and injustice towards each other.

- Some suffering is self-inflicted but not all bad things are our fault.

- The truth is that God enters and shares our suffering – we have the example of Jesus who entered the world and suffered.

*continued >*

# optional session — hot potatoes!

**byte**

continued >

- Sometimes there are no answers. Remember Jesus' cry on the cross, 'My God, my God, why have you forsaken me?'

- It's easy to assume that just because something bad has happened, God is absent. God does not hide away when suffering comes – rather he often becomes even more present and we are aware of his strength.

- God isn't some mighty dictator who does, or doesn't do, things to us.

- The world is not a perfect place. Some things appear incompatible with others.

- Suffering can sometimes be positive – people can change through the struggle.

- God does not send suffering.

- God can do everything, but experience suggests that he chooses not to.

- Jesus went through immense and unfair suffering. You cannot have Easter Day without Good Friday.

- Remember Cain, the first child of Adam and Eve, who turned away from good and became a murderer.

- Some suffering is caused by simple human law-breaking, a drunk driver who kills someone; cheap construction of houses that collapse easily; faulty wiring which causes a fire.

- God still believes in his world even when it behaves at its worst.

- An all-loving God is continually involved in creation, but he does not control everything that happens to it.

**byte**

## 2. Whose God is it anyway?

*Many people at school will be of different faiths and none. You will learn of the rich variety of belief systems, but how much of it is true? Is the Christian God the only way?*

- There are godly and saintly people in other faiths.

- Jesus is not just part of the pantheon of gods – he is the Saviour of the World.

- There is truth in all religions, but not all religions are true. For example, Muslims believe much of our Old Testament but they believe Jesus to be a prophet whereas Christians believe him to be the Son of God.

continued >

# optional session — hot potatoes!

**byte**

*continued >*

- God's redeeming love is universal.

- God's Spirit works in every human heart.

- There is only one God, but the light of Christ shines universally.

- We must and can learn from all faiths. There is a need for dialogue, comparison and celebration of similarities.

- Many people in other religions would say that they worship God and love him, therefore it is not for us to criticize. God is the only judge.

- We must not limit God's love and actions just to our world view.

- Some people believe that all godly people of any religion are drawn into the saving love of Christ.

- Most religions are about people trying to climb towards or attain God but Christianity is about God coming in search of us.

- Jesus is the only one who can forgive sins (Titus 3.5; Acts 4.12).

- Jesus says, 'I am the way, and the truth and the life' (John 14.6).

**byte**

## 3. Heaven and hell – what happpens when we die?

*With the increasing skills of science and healthcare, we are all living longer. Because we are healthier and live longer, death can seem a long way off. One thing is certain though – we will all die some day. But what happens when we die?*

- We need to realize that there is life *before* death and live well now in preparation!

- Death is not the end.

- Christians are promised 'eternal life', that we will live for ever with God.

- Heaven is a wonderful place without pain or crying.

- We will not need our earthly bodies in heaven, but we will get a makeover – that is, a body which is not as we are now, but a heavenly one.

- If we accept God's forgiveness, then we will be welcomed into God's kingdom.

*continued >*

# optional session — hot potatoes!

**byte**

*continued >*

- Think of the two thieves either side of Jesus on the cross. Both had done wrong. One of them recognized this and was offered forgiveness and 'paradise', i.e. heaven. The other, faced with total love poured out and nailed to a cross, chose not to recognize it.

- God will be our judge, and we will all be judged equally.

- God is an all-loving Father who longs for us to return to him.

- We cannot contact the dead.

- Hell is a real place. It is the absence of good.

- Hell is the total absence of God – a place where, convicted of our sin but unable to live with the knowledge of it, we depart from God's presence.

- Hell is refusing to accept the love of God even when face to face with it.

- Would a God of love consign the whole of non-Christian humanity to everlasting fire and destruction?

**backing up**

All of these questions are difficult to grasp. There are no clear answers although the Bible does help us, as does the Church. We need to keep grappling with the questions we have and to be open to understand more. Sometimes we have to live with uncertainty and unanswered questions. The Holy Spirit helps to illuminate some of these hard areas as we go through life.

**interfacing**

Invite the group to pray as follows:

- Think about someone you know who is suffering. Pray for him or her.

- Think about someone you know of another faith or no faith. Pray for him or her.

- Think about someone you know who has experienced bereavement. Pray for him or her.

- Pray for yourself, for greater understanding of God's plans for the world.

# optional session — Hot potatoes!

## 1. If God is so good why is there so much suffering?

| | |
|---|---|
| We have been given the freedom to choose between right and wrong. The story of Adam and Eve illustrates this. | Much suffering is caused by human beings' greed and injustice towards each other. |
| Some suffering is self-inflicted but not all bad things are our fault. | The truth is that God enters and shares our suffering – we have the example of Jesus who entered the world and suffered. |
| Sometimes there are no answers. Remember Jesus' cry on the cross, 'My God, my God why have you forsaken me?' | It's easy to assume that just because something bad has happened, God is absent. God does not hide away when suffering comes – rather he often becomes even more present and we are aware of his strength. |
| God isn't some mighty dictator who does, or doesn't do, things to us. | The world is not a perfect place. Some things appear incompatible with others. |
| Suffering can sometimes be positive – people can change through the struggle. | God does not send suffering. |
| God can do everything, but experience suggests that he chooses not to. | Jesus went through immense and unfair suffering. You cannot have Easter Day without Good Friday. |

# optional session — hot potatoes!

Remember Cain, the first child of Adam and Eve, who turned away from good and became a murderer.

Some suffering is caused by simple human law-breaking, a drunk driver who kills someone; cheap construction of houses that collapse easily; faulty wiring which causes a fire.

God still believes in his world even when it behaves at its worst.

An all-loving God is continually involved in creation, but he does not control everything that happens to it.

## 2. Whose God is it anyway?

There are godly and saintly people in other faiths.

Jesus is not just part of the pantheon of gods – he is the Saviour of the World.

There is truth in all religions, but not all religions are true. For example, Muslims believe much of our Old Testament but they believe Jesus to be a prophet whereas Christians believe him to be the Son of God.

God's redeeming love is universal.

God's Spirit works in every human heart.

There is only one God, but the light of Christ shines universally.

We must and can learn from all faiths. There is a need for dialogue, comparison and celebration of similarities.

Many people in other religions would say that they worship God and love him, therefore it is not for us to criticize. God is the only judge.

## optional session — нот potatoes!

| | |
|---|---|
| We must not limit God's love and actions just to our world view. | Jesus says, 'I am the way, and the truth and the life' (John 14.6). |
| Most religions are about people trying to climb towards or attain God but Christianity is about God coming in search of us. | Jesus is the only one who can forgive sins (Titus 3.5; Acts 4.12). |
| Some people believe that all godly people of any religion are drawn into the saving love of Christ. | |

## 3. Heaven and hell – what happens when we die?

| | |
|---|---|
| We need to realize that there is life *before* death and live well now in preparation! | Christians are promised 'eternal life', that we will live forever with God. |
| Death is not the end. | Heaven is a wonderful place without pain or crying. |
| We will not need our earthly bodies in heaven, but we will get a makeover – that is, a body which is not as we are now, but a heavenly one. | If we accept God's forgiveness, then we will be welcomed into God's kingdom. |
| Think of the two thieves either side of Jesus on the cross. Both had done wrong. One of them recognized this and was offered forgiveness and 'paradise', i.e. heaven. The other, faced with total love poured out and nailed to a cross, chose not to recognize it. | God will be our judge, and we will all be judged equally. |

# optional session — hot potatoes!

God is an all-loving Father
who longs for us to return to him.

Hell is a real place.
It is the absence of good.

We cannot contact the dead.

Hell is refusing to accept the love of
God even when face to face with it.

Hell is the total absence of God –
a place where, convicted of our sin but
unable to live with the knowledge of it,
we depart from God's presence.

Would a God of love consign the whole
of non-Christian humanity to
everlasting fire and destruction?

Part 3

# Living the christian life

# your kingdom come —
# god's priorities for the world

Being a Christian isn't just a private thing. It affects how we live and the choices we make. It affects those around us.

This session aims to challenge group members to apply their faith to social issues, to take on board God's priorities for his world and to share their faith with others.

## For this session you will need:

* items for the Kim's Game (see 'Warming up');
* two lots of bread dough, one with yeast and one without (see Session 9 for recipe and just omit yeast from one batch);
* big sheets of paper and marker pens;
* drawing paper and pens
* role-play cards (see p. 80).

## Kim's Game

On a tray arrange the following objects. All the objects are linked to images of the kingdom of God used in the New Testament. Have them covered up prior to the session. Unveil the objects for one minute and then cover them again. Give paper and pens to the group and ask them to recall all 10 objects in 60 seconds.

Briefly draw attention to these images, as you play or after the game. (Bible references are given in case you're not familiar with the stories.)

● A fishing net. *Matthew 13.47*

● A packet of yeast. *Matthew 13.33*

● Some sparkly jewellery (treasure). *Matthew 13.44*

● A mint imperial (pearl!). *Matthew 13.45-6*

● A party hat, invite, hooter or balloon (great banquet). *Luke 14.15-24*

● A packet of seeds (mustard if possible). *Matthew 13.31-2*

● A toy sheep (lost sheep). *Luke 15.1-7*

● A child (doll or play figure such as Duplo!) *Matthew 19.13-14*

● A bunch of grapes (vineyard). *Matthew 20.1-16*

● A coin – real or chocolate (lost coin). *Luke 15.8-10*

# your kingdom come — god's priorities for the world

## logging on

In the Lord's Prayer we pray 'Your kingdom come on earth'. Jesus uses lots of pictures and parables to show us what God's kingdom is like. This session explores the values and priorities of God's kingdom and asks us how we can build, recognize, and share the kingdom of God.

## byte

### Wonderful world

*What kind of world does God want?*

Break the group into several smaller groups giving each one a large sheet of paper and a marker pen. Spend five minutes brainstorming answers to this question and then feed back answers to each other.

## mega byte

### Doh!

Read the parable of the yeast (Matthew 13.33).

- Make two lots of bread dough about an hour before the session (one without yeast).

- Get the young people to poke and handle the dough and make comparisons between the two batches.

- What did the yeast do to the dough?

(If you made bread in Session 9 you might want to omit this activity and simply ask the group to recall what the dough looked like as it began to rise.)

*continued >*

# your kingdom come — god's priorities for the world

**mega byte**

*continued >*

Yeast changes the dough — it makes a difference to it. As Christians we are called to get stuck in and make a difference to the world in which we live.

- Ask the group to tick the issues that they care about on the handout.

- Give each person a sheet of drawing paper and ask them to design a logo for the cause they care about most. They could also work out what their main aims would be for dealing with this issue.

**byte**

## Jackpot!

Read the parable of the treasure (Matthew 13.44).

If discovering God's kingdom is like finding treasure, we shouldn't hoard it for ourselves, we should share it!

We share God's kingdom in:

- what we do;

- what we say.

How easy do you find it to talk to others about your faith?

- Divide the group into pairs and give one member of each pair a role-play card (see instructions below).

- Ask the young people to have a conversation in which the person without the card gives an answer to their partner's question.

(You could do this altogether and then feed back, or one pair at a time with the others watching and listening.)

**Instructions for role-play cards**

Make cards with one of the following questions on them:

- Why do you believe in God?

- Why do you bother going to church?

- What relevance has Jesus to me and my life?

Make enough cards for one between two.

You could add other questions appropriate to your group.

# your kingdom come — god's priorities for the world

## interfacing

Get the group to write prayers about the world, society and their role in it.

Read the prayers aloud and at the end of each one say together **Your kingdom come**.

## backing up

- When we pray 'Your kingdom come . . .' we can be part of the answer to that prayer.

- Christians can make a difference in the world, like yeast kneaded through a batch of dough.

- We can also share the news of God's kingdom with our friends and family by the way we live and the things we say.

## coming soon

Encourage the young people to:

- find out more about the cause that concerned them most;

- think about the Mother Teresa quote on the handout;

- pray for God to show them ways to share and spread his kingdom.

**Suggested timings:**

| | |
|---|---|
| Warming up | 5 mins |
| Logging on | 5 mins |
| Byte: Wonderful world | 10 mins |
| Megabyte: Doh! | 15 mins |
| Byte: Jackpot! | 10 mins |
| Interfacing | 10 mins |
| Backing up/Coming soon | 5 mins |

# your kingdom come — god's priorities for the world

## home page

Praying 'Your kingdom come on earth' means working to make the world and everything in it more like God intended it to be — beginning with ourselves.

## byte

### Wonderful world

Many things in our world are spoilt and not as God intended.

How do you think God wants it to be? Write some words on the box.

## mega byte

### Doh!

Jesus told a parable about yeast.

**The kingdom of heaven is like what happens when a woman mixes a little yeast into three big batches of flour. Finally, all the dough rises.**

*Matthew 13.33 CEV*

Just as yeast spreads through the dough and makes it springy and tasty, so God calls us to make a difference in the world.

Which issues do *you* care about? (Be honest!)

Put a tick next to all the causes that concern you:

- ○ Fair trade
- ○ Racial equality
- ○ Poverty and justice
- ○ Peace
- ○ Animal rights
- ○ Protecting the environment
- ○ Saving endangered species
- ○ Homelessness
- ○ Other?

**Which issue concerns you most?**

# your kingdom come — god's priorities for the world

## byte

### Jackpot!

Jesus told another parable about discovered treasure.

**The kingdom of heaven is like what happens when someone finds treasure hidden in a field and buries it again. A person like that is happy and goes and sells everything in order to buy that field.**

*Matthew 13.44 CEV*

If discovering God's love is like finding treasure we shouldn't keep it to ourselves!

Ask God to give you confidence to speak about your faith to others.

## interfacing

Pray that God would show you ways that you can share and spread his kingdom and that he'd open your eyes to see glimpses of his kingdom in the world.

## processing

Our contribution to society sometimes seems small and insignificant.

Mother Teresa said: 'To God there is nothing small. The moment we have given it to God, it becomes infinite.'

## do something about it

Find out more about the cause or issue that you designed a logo for. Maybe they have a website. How can you get more involved?

## coming soon

Next week:
Relationships:
All you need
is love.

# All you need is love — relationships

**For this session you will need:**

* small pieces of paper and pens for the Warming up;
* larger sheets of paper and pens;
* large paper cut into shapes of bombs, torpedoes and hammers;
* (optional) heart-shaped knick-knacks (e.g. cushion, or teddy in 'I love you' shirt – the sort of thing the shops are full of for Valentine's Day!);
* heart-shaped sweets (also optional).

## home page

One of the differences God makes to our lives is in our relationships with others. This session is all about getting on better with people and learning to love them. Sometimes that means loving *ourselves* first.

## warming up

### Email identities

* Give each group member a small piece of paper and pen.

* Invite them to design an email address for themselves that is descriptive, true (and nice!), e.g. hairylegs@big.biceps.guy or groovychick@personality.gal

* Collect them in and read each one aloud and see if the group can guess who is who.

* Get them to write their email address in the space on the handout.

This may lead to a discussion about image and self-image, differences and tolerance.

You could ask questions like:

* How easy was it to be positive about yourself?

* Were you afraid the group might laugh?

* Is it easier to put ourselves down sometimes?

* Do we sometimes hide behind an image of what we hope people will like about us, rather than show the real person?

Take the opportunity to build people up if they didn't put themselves in a very good light.

### Proceed with care

This session is about encouraging the young people to share their own lives with the group. In talking about their significant relationships it is hoped that the young people will deepen their relationships with each

*continued >*

# all you need is love — relationships

*continued >*

other. But there is also the possibility of uncovering areas of personal pain or grief. Great sensitivity is needed. No one should be forced to take part and the importance of listening to people if they *do* speak should be emphasized. It might be a good idea at this point to re-state your group's ground rules.

## logging on

Have a chat about what has happened since last week. Did anyone find out more about the causes they were interested in?

Explain that this session is all about how we get along with each other. It's about loving God and others and ourselves.

## mega byte

# Who loves you?

Either as a whole group (or in smaller groups if preferable) ask each person:

- to name someone who loves them;
- to say briefly *why* that person loves them.

*Try to keep the atmosphere light and unthreatening, but not flippant.*

You could hand round a heart-shaped cushion (or other Valentine knick-knack!) and make a rule that only the person with the heart is allowed to speak. (If group members are very shy they could then pass the heart on without speaking and simply *think* their answer.) Alternatively (or additionally) you could give everyone a heart-shaped sweet or Loveheart to suck as they speak.

Now read out Jesus' 'Golden Rule' (this is printed on the handout).

**'Love the Lord your God with all your heart, soul, strength, and mind' and 'Love your neighbours as much as you love yourself.'**

*Luke 10.27 CEV*

- Break the group into pairs.

- Invite each pair to make up a way to express this 'Golden Rule' silently, using their own sign language.

- Perform the 'Golden Rule' to each other.

Emphasize that loving God involves our whole selves — body, mind, emotions and soul. That's the way God loves us. That's the way he wants us to love each other.

# All you need is love — relationships

## Building up/tearing down

- Split the group in half, giving each group a pile of paper and some pens.

- Position the two groups at either end of the room.

- Get the group to write on separate pieces of paper things that build good, loving relationships such as 'saying sorry when you're wrong', 'listening', 'forgiving others when they hurt you', etc.

- Get each group to construct a path (or bridge) towards the other group with their bits of paper. When the paths meet, get the groups to compare the different things they have written.

- Now give them the bits of paper you prepared beforehand in shapes such as bombs, torpedoes and hammers.

- Write on these the things that destroy relationships and place them around the path.

byte

## Love your enemy

Read the story of the Good Samaritan (Luke 10.29-37). This follows straight on from the 'Golden Rule' in Luke's Gospel and is printed on the handout.

Alternatively, if you think this story will be very familiar to your group members, ask someone within the group to tell the story from memory. (You can fill in any gaps!)

Draw attention to the fact that 'Samaritan' in the time of Jesus represented the opposite of what it has come to mean today. The Samaritans were the sworn enemies of the Jews, hated and looked down upon. Jesus gives an ironic twist to his parable when he has the despised Samaritan showing kindness to the injured traveller. Our neighbour is not just the person we get along with!

Ask the group:

- Are there people at school, home or anywhere else who you find it difficult to get on with?

- How should you treat them in the light of this story?

# All you need is love — relationships

## interfacing

Ask everyone to write an email address for Jesus that expresses his unconditional love for all people. (There is space on the handout for them to write this down.) Read them out one at a time as an offering of prayer.

## backing up

God loves us! It's as simple and as amazing as that. He doesn't love us because of what we look like, or what we have achieved, or even because of our faith.

**When we were still sinners he died for us. When we were a long way off, he came looking for us. When we were downcast and lost he found us and lifted us up.**

Jesus challenges us to love and value each other with that same unconditional, free love.

**Suggested timings:**

| | |
|---|---|
| Warming up | 10 mins |
| Logging on and feedback | 5 mins |
| Megabyte: Who loves you? | 15 mins |
| Byte: Building up/tearing down | 10 mins |
| Byte: Love your enemy | 10 mins |
| Interfacing | 5 mins |
| Backing up/Coming soon | 5 mins |

## coming soon

Remind the group to check out the things to process, interface and do during the coming week.

# Handout 12
## All you need is love — relationships

God loves us! It's as simple and as amazing as that. He doesn't love us because of what we look like, or what we have achieved, or even because of our faith.

**When we were still sinners he died for us. When we were along way off, he came looking for us. When we were downcast and lost he found us and lifted us up.**

Now he challenges us to love and value everyone – whoever they are – with that same unconditional, free love.

*Write an email address for yourself that describes you –*

*Now write an email address for Jesus that describes **him** –*

### The Golden Rule

Someone who once asked Jesus about rules summarized the rules of the Old Testament in one sentence:

**'Love the Lord your God with all your heart, soul, strength, and mind' and
'Love your neighbours as much as you love yourself.'**

*Luke 10.27 CEV*

Christians are called to live by this 'Golden Rule'.

- We are called to love God with every part of our being.
- We are called to love ourselves.
- We are called to love others.

# all you need is love — relationships

## Loving your enemy

The 'Golden Rule' tells us to love our neighbour. This is the story Jesus told to answer the question, 'Who is my neighbour?'

**As a man was going down from Jerusalem to Jericho, robbers attacked him and grabbed everything he had. They beat him up and ran off, leaving him half dead.**

**A priest happened to be going down the same road. But when he saw the man, he walked by on the other side. Later a temple helper came to that same place. But when he saw the man who had been beaten up, he also went by on the other side.**

**A man from Samaria then came travelling along that road. When he saw the man, he felt sorry for him and went over to him. He treated his wounds with olive oil and wine and bandaged them. Then he put him on his own donkey and took him to an inn, where he took care of him. The next morning he gave the innkeeper two silver coins and said, 'Please take care of the man. If you spend more than this on him, I will pay you when I return.'**

**Then Jesus asked, 'Which of these three people was a real neighbour to the man who was beaten up by robbers?'**

**The teacher answered, 'The one who showed pity.'**

**Jesus said, 'Go and do the same!'**

*Luke 10.30-37 CEV*

Jews and Samaritans were enemies! Our neighbour isn't just someone we get on with.

Pray for the people you find it difficult to get on with. Ask God to bless them.

**Jesus says, 'Love your enemies and pray for anyone who ill-treats you?'**
*Matthew 5.44 CEV*

How can you do that this week?

Stand up for each other. During *Youth Emmaus* you've spent quite a lot of time with the other people in the group. Look out for each other during the week. Help other group members if you know they are having difficulties.

Next week: Your money and your life.

# Living it and giving it 1 — your money and your life

**For this session you will need:**

* Monopoly money (£1 notes) or homemade money (enough for each person to have £20) plus a large dice if using Bankrupt! Warming up activity;

* Who Wants to be a Millionaire? quiz book (or similar) if not using Bankrupt! Warming up activity;

* small sheets of paper and pens;

* selection of Fairtrade goods (e.g. chocolate, coffee, bananas, clothing, Traidcraft football, etc.) — see information on p. 91 if you are stuck;

* chocolate pennies (optional);

* large pieces of paper and marker pens;

* photocopies of Supplementary handout, p. 98 for 'Mega byte' activity.

## home page

Being Christians affects the choices we make and the way we spend our money. In this session, we begin to explore the cash value of following Jesus and living by his rules.

## warming up

### 1. Bankrupt!

* Sit in a circle and give everyone £20 of Monopoly (or homemade) money.

* Take turns to roll a dice. These are the rules for the numbers thrown:

    1 – Put £1 in the middle
    2 – Put £2 in the middle
    3 – Put £3 in the middle
    4 – Put £4 in the middle
    5 – Put £5 in the middle
    6 – Collect all the money in the middle!

* Play fast and furious for a fixed time period (e.g. 5 mins).

* Anyone who loses all their money and can't pay up is declared bankrupt and is out.

* The person with the most cash when the final whistle goes is the winner.

### 2. Who Wants to be a Millionaire?

Alternatively, get hold of a Who Wants to be a Millionaire? quiz book (or similar) and play the game in a way that is appropriate to your group.

# living it and giving it 1 — your money and your life

Ask the group how they got on praying for their enemies. Can anyone remember Jesus' 'Golden Rule'?

Explain that this week's session is about money and choices.

## byte

## Spend! Spend! Spend!

Give each person a piece of paper and a pen. Tell them to imagine you are giving them £100 to spend. Out of it they have to buy something to eat and something to wear. Beyond that they can spend it on what they like.

Ask group members to write a list of the things they would buy. (They might like to do this in pairs with £200 per pair.) Invite the young people to discuss the things on their lists.

Now ask them:

- Did any of the things you bought harm the environment?

- Did any of the things you bought rip other people off? (E.g. through unfair wages, unfair prices for commodities, bad working conditions.)

- Are there Fairtrade alternatives for any of the items you bought?

- Did you spend all £100 on yourself?

Make sure the group understand the principle of Fairtrade (products where a fair price for the grower or maker is guaranteed). You might like to show the group a collection of Fairtrade goods (e.g. chocolate, bananas, clothing, Traidcraft football, etc.).

For more information contact Christian Aid, PO Box 100, London SE1 7RT; visit the website www.christian-aid.org.uk or see their Youth Leaders' resource *m:power*. Alternatively you could check out www.fairtrade.co.uk.

Emphasize the point that how and where we spend our money affects other people's lives so we need to spend responsibly.

# Living it and giving it 1 — your money and your life

## Loaded!

**mega byte**

Talk a bit about what the Bible says about money. You could eat chocolate pennies as you do this! The Bible has more references to money than any other subject!

Jesus says our attitude to our money says a lot about our priorities and the things we really care about.

> **Your heart will always be where your treasure is.**
> *Matthew 6.21 CEV*

Throughout the Bible God's people are called to give away money.

In the Old Testament the principle of 'tithing' (or one-tenth-giving) is set:

> **Abram gave him one-tenth of everything.**
> *Genesis 14.20 NRSV*

In the New Testament the emphasis is on giving generously because our money comes from God.

> **The one who sows sparingly will also reap sparingly, and the one who sows bountifully will also reap bountifully.**
> *2 Corinthians 9.6 NRSV*

Encourage the young people to think about giving away some of their weekly or monthly allowance or pocket money. Could they give 10 per cent, or 5 per cent or even 1 per cent? Invite them to think about what would be appropriate for them.

- Now break the group into threes or fours and give each group a large sheet of paper and a marker pen.

- Invite the group to consider this scenario (photocopy it from the supplementary handout):

  **You are the managing director of a firm that makes clothing. You earn a huge salary and live in a large house with heated swimming pool, tennis courts, etc. You have a cleaner and gardener, flash car, gold card, designer clothes and are a director at a Premiership football club. In short, you have everything you could possibly want to have! Recently, you have become a Christian and have realized that the values that have driven your life do not sit comfortably with your new-found Christian faith. What do you do? Where do you look to change things? Think about your use of money, your employees, and your attitude.**

- Ask each group to list *three things* (or more, if they can think of more) that the managing director might change in order to live closer to God's way.

# Living it and giving it 1 — your money and your life

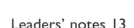

## Maker's instructions

Ask the group how many of the Ten Commandments they can remember.

Look up the list in Exodus 20.1-17.

(You could jot their answers down on a whiteboard or flip chart.)

Here is a summary of the ten 'Maker's Instructions':

1. Make God your number one. Worship him.
2. Don't put anything else before God.
3. Never use God's name as a swearword.
4. Have a day off once a week.
5. Always respect your mum and dad.
6. Don't kill anybody.
7. Be faithful in marriage.
8. Don't steal.
9. Never lie.
10. Don't be jealous of what other people have.

## Talk about God's rules for us

Emphasize that these rules are to help us and to be liberating not restricting.

Ask the young people to discuss:

- Are these ten rules enough?

- Would they add any more if they were writing the rules? What would they be?

- How many of these rules are covered by Jesus' 'Golden Rule' (Luke 10.27)?

- Is there anything they could change about their own lives in response to these ten rules?

This rap also summarizes the Ten Commandments. You could invite the group to perform it!

God gave rules for women and men
This is how it goes from one to ten.
Do not worship anyone but me
I alone your God will be.
Don't make idols, images to praise
What you make can't take my place.
Keep my name a special one
I am God the holy one.
One day a week you must keep free
Save that day to worship me.
Show respect! Love your mum and dad
This will really make God glad.
Do not murder anyone or kill
That would be against my will.
Live your lives without adultery
That sin breaks up families.
Don't steal and take what isn't yours
Pay attention to my laws.
Never lie or say what isn't true
I am God, I care for you!
Don't be greedy wanting all you see
Show content not jealousy,
God gave rules for women and men
That's how it goes from one to ten.

# Living it and giving it 1 — your money and your life

## interfacing

Being a Christian isn't just about what we believe. It's about how we live too.

As Christians we are part of God's presence in the world.

Say this prayer, slowly and quietly. (It is printed on the handout.)

**Christ has no body now on earth but yours;**

**Yours are the only hands**

**With which he can do his work,**

**Yours are the only feet**

**With which he can go about the world,**

**Yours are the only eyes through which his compassion**

**Can shine forth upon a troubled world.**

**Christ has no body now on earth but yours.**

*(A meditation of St Teresa of Avila, a Carmelite nun who wrote these words in the sixteenth century.)*

## backing up

Being a Christian isn't always easy! Sometimes God calls us to go against the prevailing tide and to make difficult choices. That's hard! God has given us rules to live by. These rules are meant to make us truly free to love God, others and ourselves.

How we spend our money and our time says a lot about who we are. Everything we have comes from God and God wants us to be generous with what we have.

**Suggested timings:**

| | |
|---|---|
| Warming up | 10 mins |
| Logging on and feedback | 5 mins |
| Byte: Spend! Spend! Spend! | 10 mins |
| Megabyte: Loaded! | 10 mins |
| Byte: Maker's instructions | 15 mins |
| Interfacing | 5 mins |
| Backing up/Coming soon | 5 mins |

## coming soon

Encourage the young people to pray, think and act as outlined on the handout.

# Living it and giving it 1 — your money and your life

### home page

Being a Christian isn't just about what we believe — it's about how we live.

### byte

## Spend! Spend! Spend!

Think about the money you spend in an average week. What do you spend it on?

Fill in the table below to see where the cash goes.

| What do I spend it on? | How much? |
| --- | --- |
| Looking good | |
| Going places | |
| Junk food and sweets | |
| CDs, books and mags | |
| Clothes | |
| Other things | |
| Other people | |
| **Total spending** | |

Jesus said that our attitude to money and what we spend it on say a lot about our priorities and the things we really care about.

> **Your heart will always be where your treasure is.**
>
> *Matthew 6.21 CEV*

Do any of the things you buy harm other people or the environment?

>

# Living it and giving it 1 — your money and your life

## byte

### Maker's instructions

Check out the Ten Commandments:

1.   Make God your number one. Worship him.

2.   Don't put anything else before God.

3.   Never use God's name as a swearword.

4.   Have a day off once a week.

5.   Always respect your mum and dad.

6.   Don't kill anybody.

7.   Be faithful in marriage.

8.   Don't steal.

9.   Never lie.

10.  Don't be jealous of what other people have.

Read them for yourself in Exodus 20.1-17.

**Do you need to change anything about the way you live?**

God gave rules for women and men
This is how it goes from one to ten.
Do not worship anyone but me
I alone your God will be.
Don't make idols, images to praise
What you make can't take my place.
Keep my name a special one
I am God the holy one.
One day a week you must keep free
Save that day to worship me.
Show respect! Love your mum and dad
This will really make God glad.
Do not murder anyone or kill
That would be against my will.
Live your lives without adultery
That sin breaks up families.
Don't steal and take what isn't yours
Pay attention to my laws.
Never lie or say what isn't true
I am God, I care for you!
Don't be greedy wanting all you see
Show content not jealousy,
God gave rules for women and men
That's how it goes from one to ten.

# living it and giving it 1 — your money and your life

## interfacing

Pray this 400-year-old meditation this week.

**Christ has no body now on earth but yours;**
**Yours are the only hands**
**With which he can do his work,**
**Yours are the only feet**
**With which he can go about the world,**
**Yours are the only eyes through which his compassion**
**Can shine forth upon a troubled world.**
**Christ has no body now on earth but yours.**

*St Teresa of Avila*

## processing

If you won a million pounds, how would you spend it? How much would you spend on other people? What would Jesus want you to do with it?

## do something about it

Find out more about Fairtrade. You could visit the Fairtrade website www.fairtrade.co.uk or Christian Aid at www.christian-aid.org.uk

## coming soon

Next week: How to share your faith with others.

# Living it and giving it 1 — your money and your life

You are the managing director of a firm that makes clothing. You earn a huge salary and live in a large house with heated swimming pool, tennis courts, etc. You have a cleaner and gardener, flash car, gold card, designer clothes and are a director at a Premiership football club. In short, you have everything you could possibly want to have! Recently, you have become a Christian and have realized that the values that have driven your life do not sit comfortably with your new-found Christian faith. What do you do? Where do you look to change things? Think about your use of money, your employees, and your attitude.

You are the managing director of a firm that makes clothing. You earn a huge salary and live in a large house with heated swimming pool, tennis courts, etc. You have a cleaner and gardener, flash car, gold card, designer clothes and are a director at a Premiership football club. In short, you have everything you could possibly want to have! Recently, you have become a Christian and have realized that the values that have driven your life do not sit comfortably with your new-found Christian faith. What do you do? Where do you look to change things? Think about your use of money, your employees, and your attitude.

You are the managing director of a firm that makes clothing. You earn a huge salary and live in a large house with heated swimming pool, tennis courts, etc. You have a cleaner and gardener, flash car, gold card, designer clothes and are a director at a Premiership football club. In short, you have everything you could possibly want to have! Recently, you have become a Christian and have realized that the values that have driven your life do not sit comfortably with your new-found Christian faith. What do you do? Where do you look to change things? Think about your use of money, your employees, and your attitude.

# Living it and giving it 2 — sharing faith

**For this session you will need:**

* items for the Warming up activity – messages and background music for Chinese Whispers, titles for Charades, or line drawings, paper and pens for Blind Copying;
* a box of Quality Street chocolates (optional);
* paper and pens;
* copies of the supplementary handout, if appropriate.

## home page

Being a Christian means being prepared to tell others about our faith. This session looks at the why, what and how of sharing our faith with family and friends. The group will even get a chance to practise doing it!

## warming up

Use one of these games about communicating.

### 1. Chinese Whispers

The group sits in a circle and some background music is played. The first person is given a written message on a piece of paper and they have to whisper the message (accurately) to the next person, who does the same to the third person and so on round the circle. The fun in the game is in how the message gets misunderstood and misheard as it goes from person to person eventually reaching the first person again in a changed state! All you, the leader, need to do is to provide the music and a supply of short written messages.

### 2. Charades

Someone is given the title of a film, a book or a TV programme and they have to act it out until somebody guesses what it is. You could give one to each person to do or allow the person who guesses to have the next go. The fun (and pain) in the game is in how difficult it can be to get your idea across without words.

All you, the leader, need to do is to provide a supply of subjects to be acted upon.

*continued >*

# living it and giving it 2 — sharing faith

continued >

## warming up

### 3. Blind Copying

Split the group into pairs. Seat them back to back so that they can hear but not see each other. One of the pair is given a blank sheet of paper and a pen, the other is given a simple picture. The person with the picture has to describe in detail what is on their picture and the other has to try to re-create the picture on their sheet of paper. (The person describing needs to give instructions of what to draw, where and how big.) Stop after 2 or 3 minutes and let them compare the originals with the copies. Each pair could have a different picture, or the whole group could work on the same one. The fun (and frustration) of the game is in how difficult it is to explain something visual or abstract with just words. All you, the leader, need to do is to provide a supply of line drawings with simple shapes, and blank paper and pens.

## logging on

Chat about last week's session and find out how group members plan to spend their millions!

Explain that the past three sessions have looked at ways in which our faith affects our lifestyle. The way we live and act shows other people that we are Christians. This session explores how we can *tell* other people about our faith — in words.

This session is slightly shorter than usual — being the last session of the course — to allow time for the 'And Finally…' activity (p.103), which is an opportunity to reflect on the course as a whole. Make sure you end well with thank yous, some good refreshments and a chance to pray for each other and your church.

# Living it and giving it 2 — sharing faith

## Made for sharing

You might like to share a box of sweets as you do this activity – as they're always better shared!

Talk briefly along these lines:

- The good news about Jesus loving us is too good to keep to ourselves – we're meant to share it. It's like treasure (remember Session 11).

- Jesus says: 'Go to the people of all nations and make them my disciples.' (Matthew 28.19 CEV)

- Talking about our faith isn't always easy. Putting deep truths into words can be difficult and talking about personal things can be embarrassing.

- We're meant to share Jesus in both the things we do and the words we say. 'Honour Christ and let him be the Lord of your life. Always be ready to give an answer when someone asks you about your hope.' (1 Peter 3.15 CEV)

Give each group member a piece of paper and a pen. Ask them to write down the *one* thing they most want their friends to know about God.

Put the papers on the floor and shuffle them. Invite each person to select a paper and read what it says.

mega byte

## What's the story?

All Christians have two great stories to tell:

- **God's story** – God's relationships and dealings with people throughout history. We call this the 'gospel', which means 'good news'.

- **My story** – how God has been working in my life and what my response to him has been.

Divide the group into pairs. (Make sure they are with people they feel comfortable with.) Explain that this is an opportunity to practise what they would like to say if someone who wasn't a Christian asked them what their faith was all about. Encourage them to be relaxed and natural and to use their own words as they 'pass it on'.

Invite group members to think back over the *Emmaus* course so far and to tell each other:

*continued >*

# living it and giving it 2 — sharing fa

## mega byte

continued >

- their summary of 'the gospel' (they might like to look back at past handouts – Sessions 4 and 10 especially);

- what difference Christian faith makes to them.

If the group feel comfortable some of them might be willing to share what they have said in pairs with the whole group.

*This would also be an appropriate moment for one of the leaders to share their own story.*

Some groups might wish to have a more in-depth discussion about sharing faith at this point – the difficulties of it, their experiences of it and ways to do it more effectively. Ideas for questions, discussion starters and resources which may help you are given on the supplementary handout.

## backing up

We only know about God's love in Jesus because someone shared the Christian faith with us. Other people will only know about the Christian faith if we share the faith with them. In the end whether people believe or not is between them and God, but we all have a part to play in making the story known.

## interfacing

Ask the group to think of *one person* they know who isn't a Christian that they would like to pray for.

Now pray this prayer:

continued >

# living it and giving it 2 — sharing faith

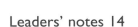

## interfacing

### A prayer about sharing faith

**Dear Father God,**

**Thank you for the good news that you made us
and want to spend eternity with us in paradise.**

**Thank you that even after we rebelled against you,
you sent Jesus to save us from ourselves.**

**We praise you for what Jesus has done for us on the cross.**

**Help us to live new lives, putting you first, and help us to pass on
the good news to other people, especially our friends.**

**Please give us courage to share our faith, and a sense
of adventure as we do it. Amen.**

## byte

### And finally . . .

Draw the course to a close with some 'How was it for you?' chat.
Here are some questions you might ask the young people.

- What was the best thing about *Youth Emmaus*?
- What was the hardest thing?
- Do you think you've changed during the course? If so, how?
- What *one* thing would you like the others to pray for you?

## interfacing

Invite the young people to pray out
loud for themselves and each other.

Conclude with a prayer thanking God
for the course and each member of
the group.

**Suggested timings:**

| | |
|---|---|
| Warming up | 10 mins |
| Logging on and feedback | 5 mins |
| Byte: Made for sharing | 10 mins |
| Megabyte: What's the story? | 15 mins |
| Backing up | 5 mins |
| Interfacing | 5 mins |
| Byte: And finally… | 10 mins |

Handout **14**

# Living it and giving it 2 —
# sharing faith

## home page

We know about God's love in Jesus because someone shared the Christian faith with us. Other people will know about the Christian faith if we share it with them.

## mega byte

### What's the story?

What *one* thing would I most want to tell my friends about God?

Write it in the box so you don't forget.

## byte

### Made for sharing

Jesus tells us that the good news of the kingdom of God is meant for sharing – like treasure. It's too good to keep to ourselves!

But sometimes talking to our friends about God is hard – so here are some helpful tips:

- When you talk about your faith, try to be yourself – use words that come naturally to you.

- Pray for God to give you opportunities to talk about him – and the right words to say!

- **'Always be ready to give an answer when someone asks you about your hope.'**

*1 Peter 3.15 CEV*

How has God been at work in me? And how has my faith made a difference to my life?

Use the box to record your thoughts.

*continued >*

# Living it and giving it 2 — sharing faith

*continued >*

All Christians have two great stories to tell:

- **God's story** – God's relationships and dealings with people throughout history. We call this the 'gospel', which means 'good news'.

- **My story** – how God has been working in my life and what my response to him has been.

Look back at your other *Youth Emmaus* handouts – especially Session 4 and Session 10.

**You could use these explanations of the gospel to help share your faith with your friends.**

And remember, it's no good knowing the Christian message if you don't live it out. Try to put into practice all you've learned during *Youth Emmaus*. People will notice the difference!

## A prayer about sharing faith

**Dear Father God,**

**Thank you for the good news that you made us and want to spend eternity with us in paradise.**

**Thank you that even after we rebelled against you, you sent Jesus to save us from ourselves.**

**We praise you for what Jesus has done for us on the cross.**

**Help us to live new lives, putting you first, and help us to pass on the good news to other people, especially our friends.**

**Please give us courage to share our faith, and a sense of adventure when we do it. Amen.**

## interfacing

Pray for one of your friends – someone who isn't a Christian. Pray for opportunities to share your faith with them.

## processing

How can I stay close to God now that *Youth Emmaus* has finished?

## coming soon

Invite a friend to come to your church or to a youth meeting with you.

# Living it and giving it 2 — sharing faith

This input is based on the work by James Lawrence in his faith-sharing course *Lost for Words* (CPAS, 1998; new edition 2002), Key Principle, Session 1. For full details see Acknowledgments page.

## Some questions to think about:

- How do people like your school friends hear about the Christian faith? (Soaps, TV programmes, hearsay from family and friends, by going to church, etc.)

- When you try to behave like a Christian are you sometimes misunderstood? Would it help to explain in words why you do what you do or think what you think?

- How do you feel about talking to someone you know about what you believe as a Christian?

- What things make it difficult for you to share your faith?

Did you know that Jesus is referred to in the Bible as 'the Word'? God's final and most accurate communication of what he is like is through the Word made flesh, his son. Jesus' ministry involved him demonstrating God's love and living a perfect life, but it also involved verbal explanation and teaching.

Jesus is also referred to as the 'image of the invisible God'. It can be difficult to describe God but he sent Jesus to 'picture' him for us. We may need to do that for our friends – to picture Christian faith so they can understand it.

### *To tell others about your Christian faith you need to:*

- Be yourself with God. Telling other people about your faith in Jesus is part of your response to what God has done for you, so let God in on the act! Pray for his help. Ask him to guide your words and actions.

- Be yourself with your friends. You don't need to be anyone else. Your story, your weaknesses and your honesty are good enough for God. Don't try to work yourself up into being someone you aren't.

- Remember that telling people about your faith is not for your benefit – it's for theirs. The Christian message is good news, so only share it out of good motives, out of friendship or because it might help. Be sensitive to other people.

# living it and giving it 2 — sharing faith

## What's your story?

These questions might make it easier for you to get to grips with what you want to share.

- What is your earliest memory of knowing God?

- When has God seemed most real for you?

- In what ways have you responded to God?

- What difference does being a Christian make to your life?

**My story – make a note of it!**

# Living it and giving it 2 — sharing faith

## God's story

God's story is summarized in the Eucharistic Prayer – the great 'Thank You' prayer that the priest says during the Eucharist.

**You are worthy of our thanks and praise,**
**Lord God of truth,**
**for by the breath of your mouth**
**you have spoken your word,**
**and all things have come into being.**

**You fashioned us in your image**
**and placed us in the garden of your delight.**
**Though we chose the path of rebellion**
**you would not abandon your own.**

**Again and again you drew us into your covenant of grace.**
**You gave your people the law and taught us by your prophets**
**to look for your reign of justice, mercy and peace …**

**Embracing our humanity,**
**Jesus showed us the way of salvation;**
**loving us to the end,**
**he gave himself to death for us;**
**dying for his own,**
**he set us free from the bonds of sin,**
**that we might rise and reign with him in glory …**

**Therefore we proclaim the death that he suffered on the cross,**
**we celebrate his resurrection, his bursting from the tomb,**
**we rejoice that he reigns at your right hand on high**
**and we long for his coming in glory …**

**Gather your people from the ends of the earth**
**to feast with all your saints**
**at the table in your kingdom,**
**where the new creation is brought to perfection**
**in Jesus Christ our Lord.**

*Common Worship: Services and Prayers for the Church of England,*
Church House Publishing, 2000, pp. 198–200.

**Some books that might help you think further about this subject:**

Phil Moon, *Hanging in There: Phil Moon's Christian Survival Kit,* CPAS/Monarch, 1994.

David Lawrence, *The Chocolate Teapot: surviving at school,* Scripture Union, 1991.

David Lawrence, *The Superglue Sandwich: if you're stuck for an answer,* Scripture Union, 1993.

additional resources

# Worship – Celebrations on the Way of Faith

This section contains three acts of worship. They are intended as rites within your Sunday worship or special one-off services. Worship with young people should always be owned by them, so encourage them to design it for themselves. The acts of worship include material taken directly or adapted from *Common Worship*.

1.   **Marking the start of the *Emmaus* journey**

2.   **A liturgy to mark a *Youth Emmaus* group member's decision to follow Christ**

3.   **A celebration of young people's faith**

# 1.  Marking the start of the *Emmaus* journey

*This is a short act of worship to be used as part of a Sunday service. It is to be used at the start of the course. The purpose of this short simple liturgy is to help the young people feel that they are recognized, supported, loved and prayed for as they explore the Christian faith more deeply.*

Invite the young people to the front of the church, where the group leader introduces them to the rest of the church.

> People of God, I would like to introduce to you these young people
> who have committed themselves to exploring the Christian faith.
>
> They are [insert names].
>
> Will you pray for them and, by your example, your love and care walk
> with them on their journey of faith?

*All*  **With the help of God, we will.**


The leader(s) of the group may then explain what the young people are going to be doing over the coming weeks.

The minister then says a short prayer for the leader(s).

> God our creator, we thank you for the wonder and mystery of human love, and of your love
> made real in Jesus. We pray for all those who will help these young people to grow in faith.
> Give them wisdom, patience and understanding, and sustain them in the weeks ahead, that
> these young people may grow in wisdom and love for you and for one another, through Jesus
> Christ our Lord.
>
> **Amen.**


The priest or group leader presents each one with a copy of the New Testament, or with a copy of one of the Gospels, saying

> N, receive the Gospel, the good news of Jesus Christ, the Son of God.

Or, if you are feeling more adventurous, ask someone in the congregation to prepare and pot a cutting for each young person.

Give the pot to each person, saying:

> This cutting is a symbol of the new commitment you are taking today.
> We pray that God will grow and nurture you in the faith.


The young people say together:

> **Dear Lord,**
>
> **Please help us as we step out in faith. Help us to discover more about you,
> about your love for us, and for your world. Guard and protect us and inspire
> us with your Spirit, and help us to grow more into your likeness day by day,
> through Jesus Christ our Lord. Amen.**

## 2. A liturgy to mark a *Youth Emmaus* group member's decision to follow Christ

*If you are not using* Youth Emmaus *as confirmation preparation you may like to create an opportunity for group members who feel ready to make a public declaration of their faith. This could take place within a normal Sunday service or within the context of a special youth service (see further suggestions). Sensitive handling is required to make sure that the young people feel comfortable and that the wider church family recognizes the seriousness of the step the young people are taking. You could schedule this service to follow Session 10 (Becoming a Christian). The following is an outline to guide you in preparing this event.*

### Introduction

The *Youth Emmaus* group leader introduces each member of the group taking part in the declaration, saying that these people have been taking part in *Youth Emmaus* and now feel ready to make a public declaration of their faith. Emphasize that this is a bold and significant step and that the young people need the love, prayers and support of the whole church family.

### Testimony

If appropriate, one or several of the young people, might like to say briefly what their faith means to them. Alternatively the group leader could 'interview' them, asking such questions as:

- What made you decide to be a Christian?

- What most attracts you to Jesus?

- How does your faith affect your life at school?

- What would you like us to pray for you?

### A prayer for the young people to say

> **Almighty God,**
>
> **Thank you for revealing your love to me**
>
> **and calling me to follow Christ.**
>
> **Help me to follow him all my days.**
>
> **Fill me with the Holy Spirit and make me strong.**
>
> **Help me to walk in your light**
>
> **and live in your love. Amen.**

Alternatively use the commitment prayer printed on the handout for Session 10:

**Dear Jesus,**

**Thank you that you are calling me to follow you.**

**Thank you that you loved me enough to die for me.**

**Thank you that you show me how to live.**

**Forgive all I've done and said and thought that has been wrong.**

**Help me to turn from selfish ways and all that is evil and to live in your light.**

**Fill me with the Holy Spirit so that I can have the strength to live as a Christian.**

**Take my life and use me to let your kingdom come on earth.**

**Amen.**

## A prayer for the congregation to say

**Father God,**

**We thank you for these young people.**

**Bless them as they take this step of faith.**

**Help us to make this church a home for them where they can belong and grow.**

**May we journey together and serve you in the world.**

**Amen.**

## A prayer for the young people and congregation to say together:

**Lord, make us instruments of your peace.**

**Where there is hatred, let us sow love;**

**where there is injury, let there be pardon;**

**where there is discord, union;**

**where there is doubt, faith;**

**where there is despair, hope;**

**where there is darkness, light;**

**where there is sadness, joy;**

**for your mercy and for your truth's sake. Amen.**

*Common Worship: Initiation Services* (Church House Publishing, 1998), p.120.

## Symbols

*Here are some suggestions for liturgical acts, or symbolic gestures that you could use in this service. Choose one that is appropriate to your context and explain to the congregation what the young people are doing and why.*

### Barbed wire and flower

Invite the young people to place a short piece of barbed wire (a symbol of the sin they leave behind) at the foot of a wooden cross (or on the altar) and to receive instead a flower (as a symbol of new life).

### Hearts

Give each young person a heart made from red paper or cloth. Invite them to pin their heart to a wooden cross (use drawing pins) or to lay it on the altar as a symbol that they are giving their hearts and selves to God.

### Names

Make a large wooden cross and cover it with white paper. Give each young person a marker pen and ask them to sign their name on the cross (or draw a cartoon of themselves) to show that they are becoming one with Christ.

### Sunflower

Make a large painted sunflower with a tall stalk but no leaves. (You could attach it to a wooden pole or mount it on a wall.) Give each young person a large green leaf and invite them to stick it onto the flower (use Blu-tack or drawing pins) as a symbol that they are growing together and are seeking to grow the kingdom of God.

### Hands

Make a large wooden cross and cover it with white paper. Provide red paint on a tray or plate (readymixed poster paint is best). Invite the young people to dip their hands in the paint and then to make a paint handprint on the cross. This is to symbolize that they embrace Christ's cross, and are, in turn, embraced by Christ. (You will need to provide a bowl of water and a towel to wash the paint off their hands!)

### Cairns

Build a cairn from stones. Give a stone to each young person and invite them to place their stone on the cairn as a waymarker, marking this step on their spiritual journey. (A similar activity is suggested in the leaders' notes for Session 10.)

## Laying on of hands

If appropriate, lay hands on each of the young people and say a prayer of blessing. If your group have soul friends invite them to lay hands on the young people too.

A suitable blessing may be the following:

The God of all grace,

who called you to his eternal glory in Christ Jesus,

establish, strengthen and settle you in the faith;

and the blessing of God almighty,

the Father, the Son and the Holy Spirit,

be upon you and remain with you always.

**Amen.**

*Common Worship: Initiation Services,* Church House Publishing, 1998, p. 183.

# 3.    A celebration of young people's faith

Part of the aim of this course is not just to help young people discover a living faith in Christ, but also to integrate them into the life of the Church. The first two liturgies are rites of passage to help young people begin the course and then to make a commitment to follow Christ. They will also help the whole church own what these young people are doing.

This youth service or Celebration of the Faith of Young People is a way of helping young people set the tone of the nature of worship within the life of the church, rather than assuming that they will fit easily into the regular diet of your church. Please also don't assume that if you have lively music bands and Power Point presentations that the young people will automatically love these and reject formality and quietness.

The following is a guide to help you plan for a youth service or Celebration of the Young People's Faith. It could be planned after the course is finished, or as part of a youth weekend. You will need a couple of leaders to help plan this, who have the blessing and authority of the minister or vicar.

A youth service could take many forms, so consider what follows as a buffet from which you can choose whatever you think appropriate – and add ideas of your own.

It is important that there is a balanced diet to this process. Therefore, there should be some singing – hymns, chants, songs – a Bible reading and some prayers.

It is also important not to be seduced into the idea that this has to be the best event ever, with all the technical wizardry of computer programs or *Top of the Pops*. It is supposed to be an authentic expression of your young people!

- First, pray!

- Second, start with a blank sheet of paper and brainstorm about what you might like to do.

- Third, work out a theme for the service. It is important that the service is of quality, and has some structure rather than the random unconnected thoughts of a group of people.

So help yourself to a selection from the buffet. (Please don't eat too much!)


## Songs of Praise/favourite readings/significant people

Choose your favourite songs or hymns and give a short reason why you like them. You can do the same with favourite Bible stories or significant personal heroes past and present (e.g. Mother Teresa, Terry Waite, Jonathan Edwards, Nelson Mandela).


## Dramatized Bible readings/parables

Choose your own reading – parables are good, and create a drama. Stories such as Zaccheus, The Prodigal Son, The Woman at the Well, The Big Catch of Fish, Blind Bartimaeus all make very good dramas! Here are some good ways to start.

- *The Dramatised Bible* (Marshall Pickering, 1989) has much of the Bible written in play form.

- You could set the stories in contemporary style, and create your own dramas.

- Create a cartoon-strip drama by dividing the parable into a series of freeze frames, then as the story is narrated, the picture changes with different poses. Use no more than ten poses to communicate the stages of the narrative.

- Dave Hopwood has written a number of books that have good sketches from Bible stories: *Acting Up* (2001), *Curtain Up* (2000), *Playing Up* (1998) and *A Fistful of Sketches* (2001) (all published by Church House Publishing) are good.

## Interview

Conduct an interview Richard and Judy style! Get a sofa and create a nice informal atmosphere à la chat show. You will need a host and two people to interview, choose someone from the church (possibly the vicar/curate or even ask a bishop!), and someone from the local community (a councillor, the local MP). Think up some questions that you would like to ask them. You will need to pre-arrange these questions – visitors should have some idea of what they are going to be asked before the event!

Alternatively, you could invite the vicar and have an 'Everything you wanted to ask the vicar but were afraid to ask session'.

## Creed/manifesto

Encourage the young people to write their own creed/manifesto for Jesus and the Church. This could be inspired by pictures such as *Seeing Salvation* (BBC) and *The Christ we Share* (USPG), and by talking about how they would like to see God in the world today, and how his nature might be made known. It can begin: 'We believe in a God who is … We believe in a Church which is …'

## Using pictures

Having something to look at greatly enhances any worship. There are many art books and websites full of colour photos. Most libraries have slide collections for projection. Here are some ideas for how to use them:

- Scan or photocopy images onto OHP acetate.

- Colour photocopies are not cheap but two or three projected on a white wall or onto screens (a white double bedsheet works well!) are very effective.

- Cut pictures from the newspaper and photocopy onto acetate for projection, or simply paste them on card and hand them round. Looking at images which reflect contemporary situations can help as a focus for prayer, worship or confession.

- Use video if you want but in general, still images work best since video can make a TV-watching people passive. Stills mean that you have to work hard to focus on them, and therefore they are more fruitful in worship and meditation.

## Using symbols

Many symbols can be used as an aid to meditation and as icons rather than idols. Remember that icons are simply windows onto God – images and symbols to help us deeper into God. Therefore use stones, feathers, candles, clay, barbed wire, flowers, bread and wine in prayer and movement. (See the previous liturgy for ideas about how to use these.)

## Testimony

(See previous liturgy.) If appropriate, one or several of the young people might like to say briefly what their faith means to them. Alternatively the Emmaus group leader could 'interview' them, asking such questions as:

● What made you decide to be a Christian?

● What most attracts you to Jesus?

● How does your faith affect your life at school?

● What would you like us to pray for you?

## Prayers

Create an environment helpful for prayer. You could try some of the following ways.

● Light some candles.

● Turn the lights down.

● Put on some ambient music, plainsong or quiet worship songs.

● Enjoy the silence!

Many young people will be happy to write their own prayers, or you could try these ways.

● Each write a prayer request on a piece of paper, fold the pieces of paper individually and put them in a bowl, mix them up and then each young person takes a piece of paper and reads the prayer out, thus ensuring anonymity.

● Make a graffiti prayer wall – tape up some sheets of lining paper on the wall and, with some big pens and paints (if you dare), people can write up their rants against God and their prayer requests and their celebrations.

● Make a large cross made out of two pieces of wood, and people can write what they want to confess on a piece of paper and nail it to the cross (you will need a few hammers and nails for this). To maintain total confidentiality, you can mark a cross in red paint on the piece of paper and then nail it to the cross.

● Use the patterns of intercession in *Common Worship* or whatever you may be familiar with – and these can be springboards into more creative prayers which are, again, written by the young people.

## Environment

Young people expect a lot of the visual and the sensory. The media revolution and our visual and electronically driven culture mean that whilst what happens in terms of content is important, the context, environment and general feel are equally vital to impact on young people with high expectations.

This does not have to be full of gimmicks. Our worship should always remain authentic and true. But we have a great advantage to start with in most of our church buildings, since they are large, impressive and beautiful with much to stimulate the senses.

We should never underestimate the power of our buildings and what they say. However, there are a variety of ideas that could be implemented from the very simple to the complex that can make a church building feel like sacred space.

It is this setting of atmosphere which will be conducive to how people feel and behave and approach the act of worship. Something which is too 'off-the-wall' will disturb and unsettle; whereas a setting that looks identical to any other service will lower expectations and there will be very little sense of the special, the new, the different and the exciting.

So how can we create or improve a worshipping environment?

### Lights

- Use fewer lights and vary the lighting combinations.

- Hire some spotlights from a local theatre company and highlight areas of the church – e.g. the cross, altar, arches or special features (an angle-poise lamp may do the trick).

- Vary the direction of lighting to create effects – e.g. a simple spotlight shining upwards to create a shadow.

- Use some coloured gels.

- Use candles instead of electric lights. Candles in large quantities can look stunning.

### Sound

- Use a CD player and vary the styles of music – e.g. Gregorian chant, Taizé music, Adiemus, Late Late Service Music (available from www.stickymusic.co.uk), or a compilation such as Classical Chill-Out.

- Hire a contemporary Christian worship band.

- Try contemporary chart music with relevant lyrics.

### Visuals

You can try some or all of the following:

- OHP visuals, both colour and black-and-white

- slides from slide libraries

- PowerPoint presentations

- computer-generated graphics

- icons

- home-made banners and posters created by the young people (maybe spotlighted)

- video clips from relevant films/TV programmes.

## Layout/Geography

Don't be afraid to use different parts of the church for different parts of the service. For example:

- See your worship as a journey — use the entrance, chancel, nave and side aisles for different sections of the service.

- Create a small prayer area in a side chapel.

- Allow people to promenade through the areas of the church and sections of worship.

- Make a Graffiti Wall in the coffee area, for people to write their thoughts and prayers.

## Smell

Smells can be powerfully evocative. Try using incense or oil burners.

# But it's so expensive!

Not necessarily! Many people have resources of their own which could be brought in, and churches also have materials that could be used to create a beautiful sacred space. Many of these suggestions come at no cost at all. Use your imaginations and don't be scared to hunt through local bargain stores for candles and other resources.

But since many of these suggestions are for a special one-off celebration, perhaps it would be a powerful symbol by the church to spend a sum of money on these celebrations as a sign of the church's commitment to their young people.

# Supervision

All this should be under the supervision of someone in authority in the church who should act as supporter, editor and guide for the whole thing. It is important that all worship that takes place in church has the blessing and permission of those who hold authority in the church. In short, the whole thing needs to have freedom and be authentic to the needs and spirituality of young people, but also to be sensitive to the nature and tradition of your church community.

# Ways of praying in *Youth Emmaus*

Throughout the course suggestions are made in the leaders' notes about ways to pray with your *Youth Emmaus* group. The course tries to make these reflective moments as creative and hands-on as possible so that praying together is an integral part of each session, rather than a few words tacked on the end. The handouts suggest things for the group members to pray about at home between sessions.

The following are some additional suggestions for ways to make prayer tactile and fun. You could use the ideas within your group, as alternatives to suggested activities or as extras – or you could suggest that group members try them at home. The activities are designed to enhance group members' experience of communicating with God. Some involve art and craft. Some are simply ideas for 'multisensory prayer'.

An excellent resource book to help your group pray more creatively is Sue Wallace's *Multi-Sensory Prayer* (Scripture Union, 2000).

## Things to make:

### Prayer beads

Make beads from air-hardening clay or Fimo modelling material. Don't forget to make a hole through the middle for threading (use a cocktail stick) before they've hardened. If you've used monochrome clay, paint the beads at a later date when they have fully hardened. (Mix PVA glue with readymixed poster paint to give a waterproof glazed effect.)

### Holding crosses

A holding cross is a smooth chunky cross that you can hold in one hand while praying. They are usually carved from wood but you could make your own from papier mâché.

- Make a cross from flat lolly sticks (cut the end off one to make it shorter) fastening them together with a glue gun or wrapped thread.

- Tear newspaper into very small strips and mix some wallpaper paste to a soft 'gloopy' consistency. Smooth layers of newspaper soaked in glue over the wooden frame until your cross is at least a centimetre thick all round.

- Leave it in a warm, dry place (such as an airing cupboard) to dry for about a week.

- Paint and varnish your cross.

### Painted stones

Paint pebbles with paint and PVA. You could make just one largish stone (the right size to hold in your palm) to hold as you pray, or several smaller ones representing people or things to pray about (like the prayer beads).

## Things to do as you pray:

### Wool strands

You will need to prepare for this activity by cutting wool of assorted colours into strands of about 15cm long – three strands per person. Present each member of the group with three strands of wool. Ask the group to move about the room to find a partner. Invite them to give one of their wool strands to a partner saying *something they want to thank God for*. Then ask them to move again and find another partner. They should give the second partner a strand of wool saying *something they want God to help them with*. Ask them to move a third time and to give a third partner a strand saying *a person they want to pray for*. (Each group member should now have three strands given them by three other people.)

Stand in a circle and ask each person to tie their three strands together into one long string. Now ask them to tie their string to their neighbours so that you end up with a big circle of wool. Everyone holds the wool circle and prays silently for the things they were asked to pray for and the leader says a concluding prayer.

### Wool web

Sit or stand in a circle. Give one person a ball of wool. Ask them to suggest something or someone they want to pray for and then throw the ball to someone else (keeping hold of the end of the wool). Continue round the circle. Every time someone suggests a topic for prayer they keep hold of the wool and throw the ball to someone else.

You should end up with a woven web of wool interconnecting members of the group. Invite them to pray silently or lead in a collective prayer.

### Stones

Try holding a stone as you pray. You could use painted personalized stones (see above), rough pebbles or polished ornamental stones.

You could suggest that the stone represents a difficulty or a 'heavy' situation, or you could make the link with God our rock who is solid and dependable. Invite group members to carry their stones in their pocket (if the stones are small enough) as a reminder that God is always with them.

### Plasticine

This is a good way of praying about God's ongoing transformation of us. Give each member of the group a blob of plasticine and invite them them to press and squeeze it. Encourage them to notice how easily the plasticine changes. Ask the group to think of something they want God to change in them (e.g. to make them more patient, less snappy, more compassionate. Invite them to pray aloud or in silence about this thing as they mould and squeeze their plasticine.

### Pictures

Cut pictures from newspapers and magazines showing people in negative and positive situations and mount them on card (or laminate them if you have the facilities). Give a picture to each group member and ask them to pray for the person in the picture (and whatever else the picture makes them think about). Play some reflective music in the background to help the group to settle.

**Text messages**

Ask group members to 'send a text to God'! What would it say? Write them down and read them aloud.

**Consequences**

Sit in a circle. Give each group member a piece of paper and a pen.

- Ask them to write the start line of a prayer that says something about God (e.g. 'Dear God', or 'Loving God') and then to fold their paper over (as in the game Consequences) and to hand their paper to the person on their left.

- Now they write a sentence thanking God for something, fold and pass on.

- Next write a sentence saying sorry for something (global or personal).

- Continue the pattern asking God to change something (in you or the world).

- Finally ask God to help with something.

You should end up with a set of five-clause prayers that represent the concerns and feelings of the group. Read them aloud.

## Some printed prayers for your group to use:

**The prayer of St Francis**

> **Lord make me an instrument of your peace;**
> **where there is hatred, let me sow love;**
> **where there is injury, pardon;**
> **where there is discord, union;**
> **where there is doubt, faith;**
> **where there is despair, hope;**
> **where there is darkness, light;**
> **where there is sadness, joy.**

**The Sarum Primer**

> **God be in my head,**
> **and in my understanding;**
> **God be in my eyes,**
> **and in my looking;**
> **God be in my mouth,**
> **and in my speaking;**
> **God be in my heart,**
> **and in my thinking;**
> **God be at my end,**
> **and at my departing.**

## The Prayer of St Augustine

Almighty God,
You have made us for yourself,
and our hearts are restless till they find their rest in you.
Teach us to offer ourselves to your service,
that here we may have your peace,
and in the world to come
may see you face to face.
Through Jesus Christ our Lord. Amen.

## Spirit of the Living God ...

Spirit of the living God
fall afresh on me.
Break me, melt me,
mould me, fill me,
Spirit of the living God
fall afresh on me.

*(Daniel Iverson)*

## St Patrick's Breastplate

Christ be with me
Christ within me
Christ behind me
Christ before me
Christ beside me
Christ to win me
Christ to comfort and restore me
Christ beneath me
Christ above me
Christ in quiet and Christ in danger
Christ in hearts of all that love me
Christ in the mouth of friend and stranger.

## God of all peace

God of all peace,
be with us.
God of all power,
strengthen us.
God of all goodness,
keep us safe. Amen.

# All-age *Emmaus*

This section is designed to act as a pool of ideas for churches who want to use the *Emmaus* material (either the Adult Nurture Course or *Youth Emmaus*) in conjunction with some provision for younger children.

For example, you may have single parents in your church who would like to attend an *Emmaus* course but have problems with babysitting. You could run the *Emmaus* Nurture Course for adults with a parallel children's activity group.

Or you might have families with both teenage and younger children. How about running all-age *Emmaus* on a Saturday morning or Sunday afternoon, or one night after school? You could have Adult and *Youth Emmaus* running simultaneously plus a children's group using the ideas suggested below. Maybe all three groups could then come together for a short time of worship and sharing – then you could eat together. The possibilities are endless!

The ideas outlined in this section are meant to be starting points rather than concrete plans. Use them in any way that suits your situation. For each session there are suggestions for a story, a song and two or three activities.

Several of the activity suggestions are taken from Kathryn Copsey's *Here's One I Made Earlier* (Scripture Union, 1995) and Christine Orme's *Here's Another One I Made Earlier* (Scripture Union, 2000). These are invaluable books for work with children.

You may find it useful to get hold of a children's version of the Bible such as *The Beginner's Bible* (Zondervan, 2001) or *The Lion First Bible* (Lion, 1997).

## Session 1

**Theme:** My God is so big!

**Story:** Read or tell the creation story using a children's version such as *The Beginners' Bible* or a book like *God's World* by Su Box and Leon Baxter (Lion First Bible Books, 2001).

**Song:** My God is so Big (*Junior Praise* 169).

*Activities:*

- Play Name Ball, Food Ball or All about You (as outlined in *Youth Emmaus* leaders' notes, Session 1).

- Make a large frieze with mountains, river and stars. Use collage materials such as tissue paper, Cellophane and coloured pasta. (You could ask each child to stick a cut-out drawing of themselves somewhere in God's world.)

## Session 2

**Theme:** God is our father.

**Story:** Read or tell the story of the Prodigal Son (Luke 15.11-32).

*The Beginner's Bible* version is good.

**Song:** God is Good (*Mission Praise* 185).

*Activities:*

● Make pig models or pig faces (to tie in with the story) – see page 33 of *Here's One I Made Earlier.*

● Act out the story using children as characters. Afterwards ask them how they thought each person in the story felt. (E.g. How did the father feel when the younger son left home? How did the younger son feel when he was walking towards home?)

## Session 3

**Theme:** Jesus – his life and ministry.

(NB There is a slight deviation here in that the *Emmaus* Nurture Course includes Jesus' death in Session 3 but *Youth Emmaus* saves it until Session 4.)

**Story:** Tell a story about Jesus from the Gospels; e.g. Jesus heals the man lowered through the roof (Luke 5.17-26), Jesus meets Zacchaeus ( Luke 19.1-10) or Jesus calms a storm (Mark 4.35-41). Mick Inkpen and Nick Butterworth's *The Mouse's Tale* (Collins Picture Lions,1994) is a lovely version of this story; or watch part of the video *Miracle Maker.*

**Song:** Jesus' Love Is Very Wonderful (*Junior Praise* 139).

*Activities:*

● Paint pictures of Jesus. (You could look at pictures of icons and talk about them first.)

● Make a Jesus banner (see *Here's One I Made Earlier*, pp. 71–2).

## Session 4

**Theme:** Jesus – his death and resurrection.

**Story:** Read a children's version account of Jesus' death and resurrection (such as that in *The Beginner's Bible*) or watch the relevant section in *Miracle Maker.*

**Song:** Thank You Jesus (*Mission Praise* 633).

*Activities:*

● Make crosses out of sticks, clay, card or artstraws. (You might like to use the wonderful resource pack *Across the World* produced by CMS.)

● Paint butterflies (as symbols of new life). Cut out butterfly shapes, fold them in half, paint one side and then press together to make a symmetrical image.

## Session 5

**Theme:** The Holy Spirit.

**Story:** Read or tell the story of Pentecost. You could use *The Beginner's Bible* or a book like *Teddy Horsley: The Windy Day* (National Christian Education Council, 2001), or *Teddy Horsley: The Rainy Day* (National Christian Education Council, 1999).

**Song:** The Spirit Lives to Set Us Free (*Mission Praise* 664).

*Activities:*

- Cut out large card fruit shapes and sponge paint them.

- Make small bowls of fruit from clay or coloured modelling material such as Fimo.

- Play a blindfolded Guess the Fruit game.

- Make mobiles with doves and flames (see *Here's One I Made Earlier*, pp. 66–9 for mobile ideas).

## Session 6

**Theme:** Prayer.

(NB Session 6 in *Youth Emmaus* equates to Session 7 in the Nurture Course.)

**Story:** Read a story about prayer such as *Teddy Horsley: Do and Tell* (National Christian Education Council, 1996).

**Song:** Prayer Is Like a Telephone (*Jump Up if You're Wearing Red*, Church House Publishing, 1996, p.28).

*Activities:*

- Draw around hands on card, cut out the shapes and write a prayer on the card hand.

- Make prayer beads or paint a prayer stone (see notes in *Youth Emmaus* prayer supplement).

## Session 7

**Theme:** The Bible.

(NB Equates to Session 8 in the Nurture Course.)

**Story:** Read a children's book that says something about what God is like, e.g. *Isn't God Great?* by Amelia Rosato (Hunt and Thorpe, 1992) or her *What is God Like?* (Hunt and Thorpe, 1998).

**Song:** Wide Wide as the Ocean (*Junior Praise* 292).

*Activities:*

- Play a blindfold game such as Blindman's Bluff or Keeper of the Keys – make the point that we need light to see our way.

- Make lanterns by folding a piece of coloured paper in two and cutting – see template and instructions on pages 130–31. Glue a cardboard tube inside the lantern and insert a rolled scroll of paper inside it with the words: 'Your word is a lamp that gives light wherever I walk.' *Psalm 119.105 CEV*

## Session 8

**Theme:** Belonging to the Church.

(NB Equates to Session 9 in Adult Nurture Course.)

**Story:** Read a story about belonging together. Jane Hissey's *Old Bear* stories (Hutchinson) would work well.

**Song:** God's Family (*Big Book Of Spring Harvest Kids Praise* [Daybreak Music 2000] 98)

*Activities:*

- Get children to paint life-size head and shoulder portraits of themselves and other members of your church family. Make them into a big frieze.

- Cut out a string of paper people (see *Here's One I Made Earlier*, p. 7). Draw faces and clothes of people in your church family onto the paper cut-outs.

- Make a family mobile (*Here's One I Made Earlier*, p. 66).

## Session 9

**Theme:** Sharing Holy Communion.

(NB Equates to Session 10 in the Nurture Course.)

**Story:** Tell the story of the great banquet (Luke 14.15-24), using *The Beginner's Bible* or read *Teddy Horsley: The Picnic* (National Christian Education Council, 1998).

**Song:** Come On and Celebrate (*Mission Praise* 99).

*Activities:*

- Play party games such as Pass the Parcel.

- Eat party food!

- Make bread (see recipe and guidelines in *Youth Emmaus* leaders' notes).

## Session 10

**Theme:** Becoming a Christian.

(NB In the Nurture Course this is Session 5.)

**Story:** Tell or read the story of Jesus calling his first disciples to 'Follow me!' (Matthew 4.18–22; Mark 1.16–20; Luke 5.1–11). You could use *Jesus Calls his Disciples* by Alan Parry (Hunt and Thorpe, 1998).

**Song:** One More Step along the World I Go (*Junior Praise* 188).

*Activities:*

- Cut out card fish shapes. Stick on sparkly collage materials (glitter, pieces of foil, sequins, etc.). Get the children to write their name on the back and then throw the fish into a big net (a strawberry net works well).

- Draw around feet onto coloured card. Cut out and decorate. Use collage materials again, or felt pens or crayons. Make a footprint trail on the wall or floor with the words 'We're following Jesus'.

- Play magnetic fishing. If you haven't got this game you can make it with a box as the tank and small card fish with paper clips fastened to them. Make rods out of sticks with string and a magnet attached.

## Session 11

**Theme:** Your kingdom come on earth.

(NB This session in *Youth Emmaus* covers similar ground to Sessions 11 and 12 in the Adult Nurture Course.)

**Story:** Tell or read the parable of the hidden treasure (Matthew 13.44) or the pearl of great price (Matthew 13.45–6). A lovely version of this story is *The Precious Pearl* by Nick Butterworth and Mick Inkpen (Collins Picture Lions, 1994).

**Song:** Who's the King of the Jungle? (*Junior Praise* 289).

*Activities:*

- Play the Kim's Game outlined in *Youth Emmaus* leaders' notes.

- Make a treasure box using the template and instructions on pages 132–3. Cut out card templates and fold along dotted line (see diagram). Cover with shiny collage materials (foil, holographic shapes, sparkly stickers, metallic ribbon, etc.). Put paper messages inside the box (e.g. John 3.16) and perhaps chocolate pennies.

## Session 12

**Theme:** Learning to love.

(NB Session 14 in the Adult Nurture Course.)

**Story:** Read or tell the parable of the Good Samaritan (Luke 10.25-37). *The Good Stranger* by Mick Inkpen and Nick Butterworth (Collins Picture Lions, 1995) is a wonderful version.

**Song:** Jesus' Love is Very Wonderful (*Junior Praise* 139).

*Activities:*

- Make heart-shaped biscuits and decorate them with icing and sweets (recipes on p. 42 of *Here's One I Made Earlier*).

- Make hearts out of modelling material such as Fimo. You could turn them into badges or fridge magnets.

- Let the children act out the story.

# Lantern template

A       B

C

X

X

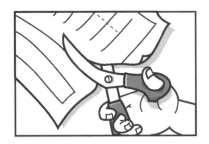

Cut out A and B around
the thick outlines.

Fold B along the dotted line,
then cut along the inner black
lines (C), away from the fold.

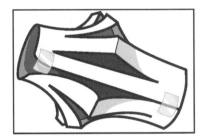

Tape sides of B together
to form a cylinder.

Tape handle (A) at the two
points marked (X). Glue
a cardboard tube inside
the lantern and insert a rolled
scroll of paper inside it with the
words: 'Your word is a lamp
that gives light wherever I walk.'

Psalm 119.105

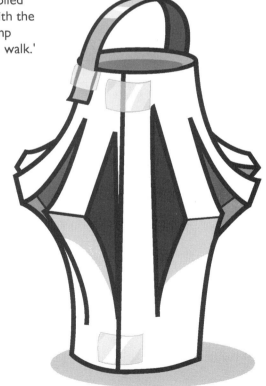

131

**Treasure Box template**

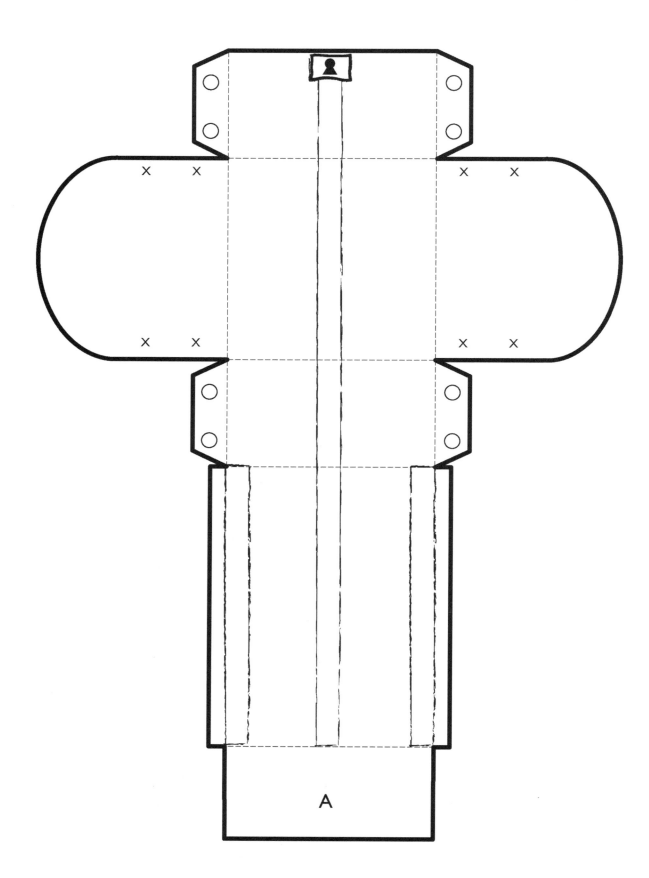

A

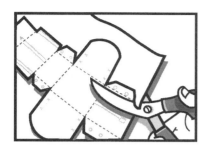

Cut out carefully around the thick outline.

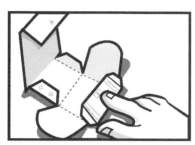

Fold inwards along all the dotted lines.

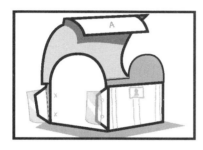

Assemble the box by sticking the 4 flaps (with 2 bolts on each), on top of the points marked X.

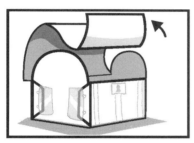

Fold flap A backwards, then tuck into the front of the treasure chest (behind the lock) to close the lid.

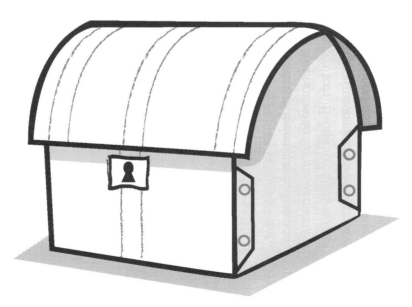

## Session 13

**Theme:** Your money and your life.

**Story:** Read a story about showing practical love such as Tolstoy's *Papapanov*, retold by Arthur Scholey as *Baboushka and Papapanov* (Lion Mini-Books, 2000).

**Song:** Stand Up, Clap Hands (*Junior Praise* 225).

*Activities:*

NB These activities are based around the meditation of St Teresa printed on the *Youth Emmaus* handout for Session 13. This meditation encourages us to use our hands, feet and eyes to serve Jesus.

- Do paint handprints and footprints. (Cover the carpet with newspaper first!)

- Make casts of hands and feet. Cover hands and feet with vaseline and then wrap in wet plaster of Paris bandage (available in craft shops). Leave ten minutes or so to set and then slide hands and feet out. Paint the casts when they dry.

- Draw and cut out large eyes from white card. Stick squares of coloured magazine pages onto the iris to make a collage.

- Play Simon Says.

## Session 14

**Theme:** Sharing your faith.

(NB Session 15 in Adult Nurture Course.)

**Story:** Read or tell the story of Jesus calling Andrew, and Andrew then telling his brother Simon. (John 1.35-42).

**Song:** One Shall Tell Another (*Mission Praise* 541).

*Activities:*

- Play Chinese Whispers, Charades or any game that involves communicating.

- Make postcards – on one side draw a picture, on the other write 'God loves you'.
  Invite the children to give or send their card to someone they know.

- Make telephones out of yoghurt pots and string. Cover the yoghurt pots with
  coloured stickers.

# The Authors

STEPHEN COTTRELL is Canon Pastor of Peterborough Cathedral and Associate Missioner with Springboard, the Archbishop's initiative for evangelism. He was one of the original *Emmaus* authors and is a well-known speaker and writer about evangelism and spirituality. His books include *Praying through Life* and *Travelling Well* (both Church House Publishing). Throughout his ministry Stephen has been involved in work with young people. He is married to Rebecca and they have three boys.

SUE MAYFIELD is a freelance writer based in Halifax, West Yorkshire. She has written six novels for teenagers and is currently working on a seventh. Recent books include *Blue* and *Reckless* – both published by Hodder Bite. Sue regularly works in schools, leading workshops and creative writing sessions. She has many years' youth-work experience and is Youth and Children's Work Coordinator at Christ Church, Mount Pellon. She is married to Tim and they have three sons.

TIM SLEDGE has recently been appointed as Mission Enabler for Peterborough Diocese. He was previously vicar of three churches in Halifax in the Missionary Diocese of Wakefield where he was also a Diocesan Evangelist. He works with Springboard and the 'Leading your Church into Growth' team. With Stephen Cottrell, he is author of *Vital Statistics,* a manual helping churches analyse and use patterns of church attendance. Tim was co-founder and leader of Sanctuary, the alternative worship service in Huddersfield.

TONY WASHINGTON works part-time for Wakefield Young People's Service. He has recently completed a Youth and Community Work course at Huddersfield University. He was previously Youth Missioner for the Diocese of Wakefield and has many years' youth work experience both on a voluntary and employed basis. He is married to Ruth and they lead the 14–18s group at Normanton Parish Church, West Yorkshire. They have a boy and a girl.

# Using the CD-ROM

## What's on the CD-ROM

The CD-ROM contains the following:

**'Handouts'** section (all PDF files):

- All the members' handouts and supplementary handouts;
- Help sheets for the Hot Potatoes session.

**'Additional resources'** section (all PDF files):

- The three liturgies from the 'Worship – Celebrations on the Way of Faith' section;
- The 'All-age *Emmaus*' section;
- '101 things to do with graphics': suggestions for using the graphics available on the CD-ROM;
- A3 and A4 *Youth Emmaus* posters;
- The *Emmaus* Resources Catalogue.

**'Cartoons and graphics'** section: All the graphics and cartoons from the handouts in both colour and black and white (in JPEG and TIFF formats – for more information see below).

**'More on Emmaus'** section: PowerPoint presentation on *Youth Emmaus* with accompanying notes.

**'Links'** section: links to useful web sites.

**'Help'** page.

## Running the CD-ROM

### Windows PC users:

The CD-ROM should start automatically. If you need to start the application manually, click on *Start* and select *Run*, then type **d:\ye.exe** (where **d** is the letter of your CD-ROM drive) and click on OK.

The menu that appears gives you access to all the resources on the CD. No software is installed on to your computer.

### Mac users:

Use the Finder to locate the resources in the folders described below. The menu application will not work on a Mac, but you will still be able to access the resources.

## Viruses

We have checked the CD-ROM for viruses throughout its creation. However, you are advised to run your own virus-checking software over the CD-ROM before using it. Church House Publishing and The Archbishops' Council accept no responsibility for damage or loss of data on your systems, however caused.

## Copyright

The material on the CD-ROM is copyright © The Archbishops' Council 2003, unless otherwise specified. All industry trademarks are acknowledged. You are free to use this material within your own church or group, but the material must not be further distributed in any form without written permission from Church House Publishing. When using images or resources from the CD-ROM please include the appropriate copyright notice.

## Handouts

The written resources require *Adobe Acrobat Reader* for display and printing. If *Acrobat Reader* is already installed on your computer, it will be loaded automatically whenever required. If you do not have it, you can install *Acrobat Reader* from the program within the **acrobat** folder on the CD, or by downloading the *Reader* from www.adobe.com.

## Graphics

The cartoons and images can be loaded into your own image editing software for resizing and printing. The files are within a folder called **images** on the CD. The CD includes both high and low resolution images; the low resolution images will be more suitable for older computer systems.

The hi-res images are in the TIFF format and are suitable for printing, projection and OHP acetates. The low-res images are in the JPEG format and are more suitable for web pages and other applications where high quality definition is not essential.

You can edit the JPEG and TIFF files with most image software. Remember that the image on the CD is 'read only'. If you want to edit the image, you should first copy it to your computer and remove its read-only attribute.

For Windows users, selecting an image from the thumbnails displayed by the menu application will prompt you to copy the image before opening it. If you select 'yes', the image is copied to a **Youth Emmaus** folder within your My Documents folder on your PC and the read-only attribute is removed automatically. The location of your **My Documents** folder varies from PC to PC but should be available as an icon on your desktop. On Windows 95 systems that predate Microsoft's use of **My Documents** folders, the **Youth Emmaus** folder will be created on your c:\ drive.

On the CD is an image browser called IrfanView. This is free for non-commercial use (see www.irfanview.com) and can be used to view the images and perform basic editing tasks such as resizing. It runs under most versions of Windows. Please note that Church House Publishing accepts no responsibility for the use of this third-party software nor can we provide support for its use.

# Error messages

You may receive the error message, 'There is no application associated with the given file name extension.' If you are trying to read one of the handouts, you should install the *Adobe Acrobat Reader* and try again. If you are opening one of the image files, your system does not have any software registered for use with JPEG or TIFF files. Install the free copy of IrfanView and during its installation make sure you associate .TIF and .JPG extensions with IrfanView.

## PowerPoint presentation

The CD-ROM contains a presentation on *Youth Emmaus* using Microsoft's *PowerPoint*. This will enable you to present the key facts about the course to groups within your church.

If you have *PowerPoint 97* or later installed on your computer, you can use it to run the presentation directly from the CD. The presentation is called **ye.ppt** and is within the **ppt** folder on the CD. If you do not have PowerPoint, install the free viewer from the same folder.

If the text in the presentation is poorly displayed, use the version of the presentation called **pngsetup.exe**. This will copy the presentation to your PC, complete with embedded fonts. Please note that the files are too large to copy to a floppy disc.

## Links

The links to web sites require an active Internet connection. Please ensure you can browse the web before selecting an external web site. These sites are not part of the *Emmaus* project and we accept no responsibility for their content.

## Further help

If you experience problems with the CD, please visit the youth section of the *Emmaus* web site at www.natsoc.org.uk/emmaus. We will post further help or support issues on this site.